PREPARE FOR REVIVAL

D0892871

Also by Rob Warner

21st Century Church

To Peter and Rachel

CONTENTS

PREFACE

Quite without warning in May 1994 a number of London churches hit the headlines. Not the usual tiresome stories of naughty vicars or unbelieving bishops. The *Daily Mail* spoke of an outbreak of "Holy Spirit Fever". *The Times* described strange eruptions of laughter, tears and mass fainting. Not surprisingly such reports led to several days of debate in the letters column, ranging in tone from the horrified to the mystified, as well as the supportive. With premature optimism, the *Church of England Newspaper* boldly announced that revival had broken out in London. *Alpha* and *Renewal* rushed first impressions into print announcing rumours of revival and a new work of the Spirit spreading like wildfire. By mid-August, *The Times* was reporting outbreaks across the country. New laughter lines began to crease the faces of Christians from the West Country to Scotland. BBC news reports took a variety of approaches, some suggesting that mass hysteria had overtaken the Church, others reporting some Christians' conviction this could become the most significant world-wide move of God since the Great Awakening in the eighteenth century.

Revival hadn't begun yet, but there was certainly something new in the air. Just as Luke recorded in Acts, with every passing week more people began to experience dynamic encounters with God. Not as carbon copied, identical experiences for every individual, but as part of a steadily increasing awareness of the presence of God – the awesomeness of his glory, the overwhelming intensity of his love, the immediate availability of his power. Church after church began to experience anew what the Apostle Peter described and promised: times of refreshing from the presence of the Lord (Acts 3:19). I had often sought inspiration from the journals of Wesley and Whitefield, but now their writings rang new bells. We began to witness firsthand, with an intensity unknown for generations, the manifestations which usually arise when the Spirit comes in power.

In mid-June I visited James Catford, my editor at Hodders, and with one voice we asked each other, "Has anything happened yet in your church?" As we shared our stories of a remarkable outpouring of the Spirit, the need for this book became clear. Someone who was fully committed and involved in this new work of God needed to provide some early reflections and guidelines. What does the Bible tell us about times of refreshing? How does our present experience compare with revivals in past generations? What are the errors to avoid and the priorities to pursue? Out of our conversation this book began to take shape.

In what follows I have included many eyewitness accounts. My hope is that the stories will build much faith, but the names of those who are not in leadership have been changed for their privacy and protection. I have also included much of my own experience and testimony over recent months. I certainly make no special claim at all for myself, for my failings are all too evident, nor for the church I lead, which is no more than an ordinary local fellowship that is seeking to go on with God. But for what I have seen and received I gladly give testimony. Refreshing and revival are an amazing gift of God. From God's glory we have received and for God's glory alone we tell the story.

The value of firsthand testimony is clear, for each of us has to make our own decisions before God. Will we enter personally into all that God is doing in these days? Will we allow God to do whatever he likes, in us and through us, with no escape clauses? If we will, then what we have seen, received and enjoyed so far is just a tiny morsel of the abundant outpouring which God intends for his Church at the end of the twentieth century.

As ever my special thanks go above all to my dear wife, Claire, without whose support I would not have been able to write this book at all.

Rob Warner
August 1994

FOREWORD

The Church of Jesus Christ is in a time of change unprecedented in our lifetime. On the discouraging side is the lack of support and dwindling numbers experienced by the denominational bodies; a growing bewilderment in the face of the increasingly obvious and serious national – even universal – issues of unemployment, divorce, crime, ecological disasters and all the implications for families and society these have. Perhaps even more significant is the sense of meaninglessness felt by so many young people with a growing cynicism about the ability, or indeed the desire, on the part of anybody to do anything to alter the situation.

On the other hand, there are in the Church many very exciting and encouraging signs of new shoots springing up all over the place. Without attempting to list them all, perhaps it is worth drawing attention to a few. The section of the Church known in traditional churches as 'the laity' – the vast majority of the Body of Christ – is gradually breaking free from the clerical strongholds that have dominated it for so long. Laypeople want to be part of the purpose of God today and function as the Body of Christ, an army ready to speak, intercede, minister, heal and bring the Kingdom of God and the love of Jesus Christ to the millions amongst whom they live.

There is a new longing for spiritual gifts and a recognition that we need everything we can get if we are to achieve anything of lasting spiritual value as we live out the life of Christ. There is a growing understanding of the place of small groups, home groups, intercessory and other groups, in the life of the Church. There is a wonderfully exciting desire to get on with evangelism, to see people brought under the mastery of Jesus Christ. There are, for example, somewhere between six and seven hundred Alpha courses that I know of now running all over the country and the number increases weekly. There is an increasing and healthy suspicion of and impatience with denominationalism – the desire to see one group grow at the expense of another – as we are all being overtaken by the longing to see God's Kingdom grow with all the multi-faceted creative variations that God seems to love.

Above all there is a new and real hunger for God. It is not always expressed as such, but takes the form of a desire to discover and experience the love of God and all that a deep relationship with Him can mean, when a person's mind, heart, soul, spirit and body – every part! – is caught up in the life God always intended us to enjoy, and which Jesus Christ went to the cross to enable us to receive.

All these encouraging signs are the work of God's Holy Spirit wooing His Church, although some aspects of His activity seem easier for us to understand than others. In recent months this has become more obvious. The changes taking place in the Church today have already attracted a great deal of comment and raised many questions. Rob Warner's book is extraordinarily helpful and well researched, taking us step by step through the questions and pitfalls which many of us have been attempting, with God's help, to navigate recently.

We can only pray and dare to believe that, as we enter into what God is doing today, we too, like our forefathers, may see the land that is very far off and experience full-scale revival in our times. Let's hope so!

Rev'd Sandy Millar
Holy Trinity Brompton
October, 1994

Chapter 1

HOLY SPIRIT FEVER

"I was prayed for this morning," said Peter, as we strolled towards my car. We had just left a meeting of the younger leaders' forum at the Evangelical Alliance in South London, where the nearest place to park is down back streets some distance away. Nothing unusual about being prayed for, I thought, although Peter did seem to have a new air of confidence and authority.

"What's more," he added, as I turned the key in the ignition, "I fell over, and spent the next ninety minutes on the floor. Most of the time I was simply receiving from God, but those praying also prophesied over me, and the Lord has really spoken into my life and ministry."

I've know Peter for years and one of his characteristics had always been a certain diffidence about himself, despite the fact that he is widely recognised to be a highly gifted teacher, pastor and evangelist. As Director of Training for Oasis he had been visiting one of his students on placement at Queens Road Church, Wimbledon. One of the leaders there had told him about a new season of blessing in their church and then offered to pray for him. I was seeing the immediate results and I was impressed. I respected Peter's judgment, and knew he wouldn't jump into the latest fad just for the sake of it. Nor is he the sort who would easily fall prey to emotional manipulation or hysteria. I was more than impressed: I knew at once that what Peter had received, I wanted.

There was no time for Peter to pray for me when we got home. It was late afternoon and we both needed to catch some brief moments with our children before the evening appointments came around. Before we parted, Peter gave me copies of some guidelines from a church in Toronto, the Airport Vineyard, where this new outpouring of the Spirit had been experienced continuously since late January. He also suggested that I phone Norman Moss, Senior Pastor at Wimbledon, to find out more.

A couple of days later, after battling unsuccessfully with their church's fax and answerphone, I finally got hold of Norman at his home. Norman is a quiet, thoughtful and unassuming man, who over many years of service has built up in Wimbledon a really good fellowship, Baptist in origins and now linked to New Frontiers. It's a church my wife and I would gladly join if we were living in that area. Like Peter, he is a man I know personally, whose judgment I trust and whose ministry I admire.

Norman didn't seem surprised to hear from me. The phone lines to Wimbledon were already buzzing regularly with calls from church leaders wanting to find out more. He told me about what was happening in their church. The move had been triggered by a prophetic call to repentance, given through tears by a young woman two weeks before Pentecost. When Norman asked her why she was weeping, she explained that she saw a vision in which the whole church was repenting before God and then the people joined hands together around the building in prayer. Norman decided to act upon this vision, and called the congregation back to pray. He was naturally relieved to discover that the vision of hands joined in prayer involved standing around the walls inside the building, rather than out on the streets. As the prayer time extended late into the evening, some who had gone home earlier heard what was happening and returned to join in prayer.

Above all Norman told me about his visit to the Airport Vineyard, Toronto. Having heard a great deal about what God was doing, he had travelled to Canada. He explained that the Airport Vineyard had been having meetings every night of the week except Mondays. God was visiting them in great intensity, bringing refreshing to believers and drawing an increasing number of non-Christians to conversion. In

Norman's words, while he has never been quick to show external manifestations under the influence of the Holy Spirit, his wife, Margaret, spent more time in Canada on the floor than upright. While Norman felt that he had met with God in a powerful way, he was rather embarrassed by the small and curious physical manifestation he had received: a strange twitching in the stomach. He told me of others who wept and laughed under the presence of God. One visiting minister was looking on sceptically when the Spirit came upon him. It was as if his bones had begun to dissolve. Gradually but irresistibly, he began to slide down the wall against which he had been leaning, until he was prostrate before the living God.

On Norman and Margaret's return home, they found they were ministering in greater power than ever before. Leaders at a Wimbledon church plant were unable to preach or lead worship, falling spontaneously to the ground, overcome by the glorious presence of God. When Norman prayed at an elders' meeting, the Spirit came in great power. One man who had been cautious was suddenly and mightily blessed by God, filled with joy and awe. There followed what Norman described as one of the most earnest and significant times of intercession he had ever experienced. The church had now started a late night meeting on Sundays to cope with the numbers streaming forward to know more of God. There were queues before the meetings, and over 200 people had ended up lying on the floor receiving prayer.

It was not that lives were being touched in ways never seen before, but that the work of God was now advancing with a new intensity. They were seeing many deep works of repentance, with tears and substantial changes in lives. Others were so profoundly refreshed in God's presence that they were caught up in torrents of laughter. He told me of believers who became drunk in the Spirit, legless under the blessing of God. A couple in the police force were staggering out of one meeting, leaning on one another for support. Looking across, Norman simply said, "God bless the police!" Instantly they both fell to the ground once again. Many people were recommitting themselves to Christ. The church was also seeing a steady increase in the number of new converts.

So what had Norman learnt from the Airport Vineyard? Above all, the sovereign mercy of God was breaking out in fresh outpourings of the Spirit, beyond anything seen in Britain for generations. In addition, Norman identified two key methods in the Toronto church. Firstly, in every meeting they called to the front two or three who had recently been mightily blessed. These willing recruits would give their testimony of what God had been doing, and then they were prayed for again. Norman interpreted this practice as lighting new fires from warm coals, building faith in the congregation by a verbal witness and visible demonstration of the powerful presence of God. Norman's second key observation was the Airport Vineyard prayer team's practice of "soaking in prayer". There was no hasty production line prayer of blessing, rapidly moving on to others. Rather, the team were prepared to spend as much time praying for each individual as they needed. In particular, when someone receiving prayer fell to the floor, the prayer team continued to minister to them. "We used to treat falling down as a completion of blessing," Norman explained. "Now we realise that at this moment God may have only just begun."

When Norman finished describing his visit to Toronto and the subsequent breakthroughs at Wimbledon, he paused for a moment, giving me time to respond. He was used to church leaders expressing initial reservations or even fears. They naturally wanted to make sure that this was no emotional hysteria or foolish excess, and that it would not result in untold damage within their church. He also knew that I like to check things out with Scripture, and am by nature always cautious about rushing into the latest spiritual fashion. As a result, Norman was pleasantly surprised by my immediate reaction.

"Do you have any questions?" he asked.

"Only one," I replied. "When can I receive?"

My ready response came in part from my friendship with Peter and Norman. Knowing them so well, I had every confidence that their new encounters with God were genuine and significant. What's more, I felt that God had been preparing both me as an individual and also our church for something more. The roots of this preparation went back some months. I had been given a prophetic word during the European Charismatic Council meeting in Budapest in autumn 1993: "Let Elisha seek a portion of the Spirit of Elijah." As a result, the older leaders in renewal, who naturally form the majority of the Council, prayed for their younger colleagues, seeking a mighty anointing upon the emerging generation.

As for the preparation of the church, during a church weekend away in 1993 that otherwise had been frankly disappointing, the highlight for me was a late night prayer meeting at which we had prayed ardently for God to increase the outpouring of his Spirit upon us. At a half night of prayer in January 1994 expectancy had increased when several Scriptures were given that stressed God's empowering presence. For me personally came God's promise to Moses: "My Presence will go with you, and I will give you rest" (Exod 33:14). For the church there were a number of promises concerning God's resolve to manifest his presence powerfully with the result that his life would flow out vigorously into our city and nation (1 Kgs 8:29; Isa 54:2–3; Ezek 43:7; Ezek 47, especially v 9; Zech 10:1, 3). In the coming weeks I discovered these same verses had been given recently to a number of other churches too, which seemed promising.

The three most immediate preparations had all come through the preaching over the previous few weeks. On 24 April, I was due to deliver the last message in a series from Isaiah. Early in the week, as I re-read the whole of the book once again, I became convinced that the Lord wanted me to preach on Isaiah 58:9–12. I began the message by stressing the need to do away with negative and critical attitudes among Christians and the need to spend ourselves for the sake of the poor. Then I turned to God's promise to do for us what we cannot do for ourselves, sending streams of living water into our spiritual dryness to make us like well-watered gardens, like springs whose waters never fail. Finally I spoke about a generation of restoration, not only the generation that returned from Babylonian exile and saw Jerusalem liberated and rebuilt, but also the generation who will see the spiritual and moral restoration of Britain and Europe, when God brings revival upon our continent.

During the sermon, which was preached at both our morning congregations, I sensed a powerful anointing, and the people seemed greatly moved and touched by God. Several were caught up in quiet weeping. Others stayed after the service to continue to pray, some requesting prayer, some praying on their own. We discovered over the coming weeks that what rang the most bells was the promise that God would make us like well-watered gardens. As I preached those words the Holy Spirit began to stir up a deep longing in many hearts, an almost painful ache for a closer walk with God. Many began to realise how much they were going through the motions, drifting far from intimacy with God, growing dry and barren in their inner being.

On 15 May I preached to the evening congregation on Colossians 2:6–7:

> So then, just as you received Christ Jesus as Lord, continue to live in him, rooted and built up in him, strengthened in the faith as you were taught, and overflowing with thankfulness.

Once again I felt a particular anointing in the preaching, and at the end of the message I invited any Christians who wished to express a fresh yielding to Christ to come to the front. We began to sing a song of response and almost immediately the congregation swarmed forward, leaving only about six in their seats. With tears in my eyes, I stepped down from the platform to join the people before God. Together we yielded our lives afresh to the Lordship of Christ. Some wept, many knelt. It was a sacred and unforgettable moment of submission in the presence of our risen Lord.

The following Sunday was Pentecost, and when I finished preaching in the evening the room was filled with a sense of earnest longing after God. I invited the congregation to pray in small groups while I called the elders to join me at the front. "We need to pray together," I explained, over the buzz of prayer from the people. "I know God is at work powerfully tonight, but I'm not sure what we should do next." After praying and discussing together, the elders raised hands in blessing over the congregation, and prayed for a mighty flood of the Holy Spirit to be released, not only on those present but also on the whole church.

Never before had I seen such a widespread seriousness of seeking after God, such a thirst for more of the Holy Spirit. What's more, the elders' spontaneous public prayer seemed to me to be crucial and strategic, opening a way for God to work among us in unprecedented power. It was the very next day that Peter told me he had been prayed for, and a day or two later that I spoke with Norman. These events set the context for my enthusiastic response to Norman's question. I felt God had been warming us up, preparing us for a fresh visitation of the Holy Spirit, and I was eager to receive.

On the Thursday evening that week a joint meeting was planned for our deacons and elders. They do most of their work as separate teams, and only meet together formally two or three times a year, to discuss a major issue or to pray together. On this occasion there was no major issue on the agenda, and so it was easy to invite Peter to join us. Once again he described his experiences that Monday, and went on to describe various prayer meetings he had led that week, both at Oasis and at Spurgeon's College. Many people had met powerfully with God as Peter prayed for them, several of them falling to the ground, overcome by the presence of God.

As Peter spoke his right hand began to shake. I had known him for nearly fifteen years, but I had never noticed a nervous twitch before. I knew him well enough to be sure that he would never do such a thing for dramatic effect. The only possible explanation was that the trembling was involuntary, prompted by God. In a way I didn't yet understand, this was clearly a sign that the Spirit's power was resting on Peter. Not wanting to force the leaders into something they were not yet ready for, I asked whether they wanted to discuss other matters or have Peter pray for us. No hesitation was voiced and we turned to prayer. When Peter invited anyone who wanted personal prayer to step forward I knew there was only one thing for it: I needed to be prayed for first.

Up to that moment I had never fallen over as a result of prayer. The first time I was filled with the Spirit was at St Michael-le-Belfrey in York, during a communion service. David Watson laid hands on me, and I returned to my seat filled with joy. That night I lay awake with a wonderful sense of God's presence and a burning sensation running through my body. But in those days no one fell over at St Mike's. It just didn't happen. And for me it had never happened since. Sometimes I'd felt rather weak at the knees, and I'd seen some people fall over when I prayed for them, but I was wary. I didn't want anyone to push me over, nor did I want to conform to some kind of emotional pressure. Nor, to be absolutely frank, did I want to make a fool of myself in public. Soon after Peter began praying for me I knew that I was going to fall. There was such a weight of God's glory upon me that I could stand upright no longer. My strength sapped away until all I could do was fall to the floor. At first I was simply overcome by the glorious presence. Then it seemed that God spoke to me, clearly but firmly: "Let me be God."

As a church leader I had grown accustomed to making things happen, praying for those who are ready to receive, trying to provide support to those who may feel left out or threatened. But here was God moving in power and commanding me to stay on the floor. As God manifested his glory to me he was also keeping me out of the way. No one could possibly give me any credit for what God was doing that night, nor could they blame me for it. All I was doing was lying on the floor.

After a while my self-consciousness began to get the better of me and I moved to get up. But I couldn't. I felt glued to the floor. And so I rested in God, realising how tired and drained I had become in the tasks of ministry, how much in need of the awakening presence of God. Finally I felt I received permission to get up and walked slowly back to my seat. Peter was making slow headway with the queue of leaders seeking prayer, despite the able help of one of our elders. "Do give a hand when you're ready," he asked. I sat back in my chair, expecting to be praying for others quite soon. But further waves of God's presence came upon me. My head sank to one side as I continued to rest in the Spirit. My sense of God's glorious presence continued to be heightened as never before. My ability to get up and minister to others was non-existent. Like many who spend a lot of time giving out to others, I need to learn more about receiving. That evening God took me right out of the action, rested his glory upon me, and obliged me to receive, not just for a minute or two, but for what seemed like hours.

The next Sunday the Spirit began to come upon our services in power. Claire found that I was not home for lunch before 2 p.m. That evening, prayer continued until about 10.30 p.m. Over the next few weeks God intensified this new work among us, turning up the heat steadily so that more and more began to receive. We were part way through a training course on Tuesday evenings and when I prayed at the end of the next session, someone immediately dropped to their knees and began to repent before God. In case this is customary elsewhere, perhaps I should explain that this had not been the normal practice in our church! The following week the presence of God came down even more abundantly upon us and everyone in the meeting was powerfully touched; some fell peacefully to the floor, some sat rapt in God, some were weeping before God, others trembled and shook in God's presence. At midweek prayer meetings, after we had prayed through any critical needs of the moment, I began to answer questions about this new work of God, gave some teaching, and then we turned to testimony and prayer. At the first prayer meeting many fell down as they received personal prayer. At the next, many fell spontaneously as God's weighty presence came down upon the room. Soon we experienced our first eruption of infectious laughter, first one or two, then many together bubbled up with overflowing joy in Christ.

Roger Forster preached for us at the beginning of June and gave a world perspective: he had recently spoken at conferences in several countries where the Spirit was moving in increasing power, bringing repentance and conversions, joy and laughter, and also an increased level of healings. After the service Roger prayed for John Taylor, director of Youth With a Mission for London and South East England. John first joined our church about four years ago and I have always appreciated the impact of his words of knowledge, his zeal to pray for others to be filled, and his ministry of healing and deliverance. John had already been a part of prayer meetings in YWAM where they had earnestly sought the Lord for a fresh outpouring, with many receiving a gift of laughter. As Roger began to pray, the Spirit came on John with such power that he crashed to the ground like a felled tree. No catcher could have restrained his descent. During the last few months God has increased the anointing upon John, deepened his thirst to know ever more of God, and used him more mightily than ever among us. As I write, John led worship last Sunday evening with Heidi, his wife. During the worship we nearly lost our preacher, who was all but overcome by the presence of God. After the sermon, when we moved into a ministry time, most of the congregation received personally from God, many of them ending up on the floor. John and Heidi, Claire and I, along with others in the prayer team, moved freely among the people, sometimes praying alone, sometimes together. At one time I prayed for John, later he prayed for me. The release of the Spirit continues to increase weekly, not just a trickle but a flowing torrent of the love and power of God.

Sunday by Sunday we have seen a steady increase in people coming forward for prayer. More pleasing still have been their reasons. Many declared a deep thirst for God. Many began to repent, to submit to Christ's Lordship, to seek his love and receive his power. Deep sins and hurts began to be exposed and dealt with by God. The overwhelming sense of God's love enabled some to speak openly for the first time about deep wounds, such as sexual abuse or coming to terms with a suicide in the family. Demons could no longer hide before the manifest presence of God, and just as in the Gospels and Acts, they began to rise up to the surface and were dealt with in the name of Jesus. One man who had dabbled in many kinds of drugs and had always struggled to sustain his Christian commitment came forward for prayer. When the Spirit came upon him, it was as if he had been struck by lightning. He was poleaxed. Some time later when he began to come round he said, "Rob, I've experienced many illegal drugs in my time but I have never, ever experienced anything half as powerful as the Spirit of God. Look at me, I'm still shaking on the inside." We wait to see what the long-term results may be in his life.

Some intended to come forward for prayer but couldn't make it to the front. One woman got halfway, felt overwhelmed by God's presence and sank into a chair, resting in the Spirit. One young man was clearing up the microphones when God's presence came upon him. It was impossible for him to stay on his feet, so he sat down to wait for prayer. When his turn came to be prayed for he was still unable to stand, overcome by his unworthiness before God. He knelt weeping before his Lord, and later fell face down on the carpet. One man was coming forward for prayer when, in his own words, "I hit what can only be described as a wall of joy." Suddenly red-faced he began to laugh with joy, a side-splitting laugh that left him rolling on the floor.

Some come forward without knowing why. As a rule Tim only comes on Sunday mornings, but one evening he knew he had to come. When we turned to prayer I knew the Spirit was moving upon his life, but I resolved to wait for him to make a specific request for prayer. Finally he could remain seated no longer, and as he came forward his need came into focus. Although in principle Jesus was still his Lord, in practice the demands of career and family had squeezed Jesus to one side. He prayed in confession and recommitment and then we prayed for him. Public school and Oxbridge and enormously successful in business, Tim is by no means the kind of man to cry easily, but that evening the tears flowed until his cheeks shone bright, his eyes grew red and his shirt became soggy. After standing in prayer for a long time he returned to his seat, where he continued to be caught up in God's presence. From time to time I checked how he was getting on. He was well out of it, tearful and groggy but at peace in God's presence. He was like this for about ninety minutes, and afterwards I asked him what was going on. "Sometimes I have felt the warmth of God's presence," he explained, "but only for a moment or two. Tonight I felt enfolded in the warmth of God and it just went on and on. In fact the only word for it is 'drunk'. When I looked at my watch I was astonished at how long it had lasted. Nothing else mattered except knowing God's presence and allowing him to reorder my life."

Others express a very definite prayer request. One man came confessing a desperate spiritual thirst. His life was so busy he was struggling to find time for God. Within moments he fell to the floor, but then his activist nature began to get the better of him and he quickly started to pick himself up. As we turned to pray for him again he sank back to the carpet, and at last gave sufficient time to receive at depth from God.

One engaged couple came forward with wonderfully matching requests. Pam came confessing that in the delight of her new-found love for Colin, she realised that Christ was no longer first in her life. Pam is a doctor from a fairly safe and respectable Anglican church. I expected a quiet and restrained response, maybe a few silent tears. Soon after beginning to pray she collapsed on to the carpet. Colin had other needs that God dealt with that evening, but he too renewed his commitment to putting Christ first in his life. At first he wept like a baby before his Father in heaven, then he sank to the ground as he received a fresh touch of the love of Christ. Colin and Pam hadn't consulted about their requests beforehand, so when they swapped notes they were delighted. A few weeks later they told me that their prayer life was much improved and so was their relationship. When Christ is put first, human love grows stronger.

While in the past many have received prayer once and then returned to life as usual, we have begun to learn the value of soaking in prayer. Since God is infinite, his resources of love and power are naturally limitless. This means there is always more for every believer to receive. When Sarah was prayed for in her home group she grew weak at the knees, felt awkward and resisted God's prompting. The next Sunday she knew she needed to ask for prayer again, this time with no strings attached. Under the power of God she fell to the floor, and has done so since at almost every meeting. At home she falls to the floor when she prays. In her lunch hour she prays at work, often with the same result. At one midweek prayer meeting she was still resting in God so late at night that I eventually left her with the keys to lock up on her way home. Although on that occasion the entire evening was given over to receiving, very often she is used mightily in prayer for others once she returns to her feet. Sarah has an itinerant speaking ministry and is also gifted pastorally. In this fresh outpouring, the Spirit is giving her such an intense sense of the presence of God that her speaking and pastoral gifts are being used more powerfully than ever before.

The testimonies that have resulted are even more pleasing and significant than the prayer requests. Later in this book I will consider the biblical signs of a powerful work of the Spirit. For the moment I will name but a few of the results we have regularly witnessed: a new love for Christ; a new appreciation of his cross; a new hunger for the Bible; a rededication to discipleship; a new awareness of God's presence; an overflow of joy; a release from deep hurts and habitual sin; a new passion for the lost. To adapt the words of a well-known British commercial, "Only the Holy Spirit can do all this!"

While God continued to increase his work among us, I began to hear daily of more churches in the London area that were being touched by this new wave of the Spirit. Anglicans, historic free churches and new churches were all involved, demonstrating afresh that God has no denominational favourites. As a result I phoned Joel Edwards, a Pentecostal pastor and a senior leader in the Evangelical Alliance. "Joel, I have some great news. The Spirit is being poured out upon Herne Hill. And it all began just one week after you preached here!" Joel chuckled at his prematurity. "Joel, this is breaking out all over London, and I want to encourage you to give some space to it at the London leaders' prayer meeting on July 6th." I simply had no idea when I spoke to Joel how significant that meeting would prove to be.

The London leaders' prayer meetings had been running for eighteen months or so, co-ordinated by Joel Edwards and Lyndon Bowring, usually taking place either at Holy Trinity, Brompton or Westminster Chapel. To me, the two most striking things about these meetings had been the welcome presence of black Christian leaders in much greater numbers than I had ever seen before and also the unity of earnest prayer for God to move upon his church in our nation in reviving power. Joel got back to me a few days later to confirm that they were indeed planning to focus on the new outpouring. As a result, he asked me to provide a brief biblical and historical perspective on what was going on. He and Lyndon had also arranged for eyewitness accounts from two of the churches most profoundly affected thus far, Queens Road Church, Wimbledon and Holy Trinity, Brompton.

There was an extra expectancy in the prayer meeting that day. After I had spoken, Norman Moss repeated the testimony he had shared with me over the phone. However this time his wife Margaret spoke too, both of her own power-ful encounters with God and also of others in their church, from young children to the elderly. Then Norman prayed for her. She shook more and more vigorously, sighed with a smile on her lips and then sank to the floor, still shaking quite violently under the powerful anointing of God.

Sandy Millar then gave the perspective from Holy Trinity, Brompton, in his typically self-deprecating manner. On Tues-day, 24 May, he had been attending a meeting at the Evangelical Alliance when he received an urgent phone call from a member of staff at Holy Trinity, Brompton. The message was simple: Nicky and Pippa Gumbel had met that morning with John and Eleanor (Elli) Mumford and a number of other church leaders, following Elli's trip to the Airport Vineyard. John Mumford began his ministry as an Anglican and then moved to the Vineyard, and with Elli he now leads the South West London Vineyard in Putney.

As Elli prayed for a fresh infilling of the Spirit, everyone present was touched by God. Suddenly Nicky recalled the staff business meeting at Holy Trinity and scooted back to the church offices. He'd missed the meeting, but the others asked him to close in prayer. Nicky prayed for the Spirit of God to fill everyone in the room and now Sandy was hearing the instantaneous and dramatic results: "I thought you ought to know that the entire staff are lying on the floor."

Wondering what the others at the Evangelical Alliance meeting might make of such behaviour, Sandy played for time. "And is it a good thing?" he asked.

"Oh yes, it's very good," came the reply.

"Well, if it's so good, how come you're not lying on the floor like everyone else?"

The explanation may have been a little pained: "I am on the floor, and I cannot get up! I have just crawled across the office to the phone in order to let you know what's happening!"

Sandy returned to his committee meeting, while prayer in the Holy Trinity offices continued till after 5 p.m. Some simply walking past the room were affected. Those in other offices were brought up to date and prayed for, with the result that many of them also fell to the floor.

The next Sunday morning, 29 May, Elli Mumford spoke at Holy Trinity, Brompton. She gave an account of her recent trip to Toronto, speaking simply but eloquently about her own spiritual bankruptcy as she travelled to Canada. She went expectant and needy, and came face to face with a church experiencing a wonderful release of freedom, joy and power. She told of Christians restored and people coming to faith. She described a release of joy in her own heart, a deeper love for Jesus than she had ever known before, a greater appetite for ministry than she had known for years. When Elli finished speaking her words had won over the people's minds and hearts. When she prayed for the Holy Spirit to come, the results were dramatic.

Silence slowly melted into tears and then into laughter. Many who came forward for prayer fell to the floor as they received. When the children returned from their classes, many of them also met powerfully with God. The ministry time continued till after 1.30 p.m. That evening Elli was asked to give the same talk, so wonderful had been the impact in the morning. Once again the Spirit came in power and many were touched, weeping, laughing and falling to the floor. Then more than a hundred visitors from other churches came forward for prayer. As the ministry time extended, many rows of chairs had to be moved. Such was the response that prayer continued until late that night.

Seeing such an outpouring, Sandy concluded that the only sensible option was a swift visit to Toronto, which he made that same week. The next Sunday, 5 June, Sandy was back in action at Holy Trinity, Brompton. Testimonies from Nicky Gumbel and others who had been touched led into further prayer ministry. So overwhelming was the response that a planned communion service had to be cancelled. That evening Holy Trinity was packed with 1,200 people. Once again so many ended up on the floor that many chairs had to be removed. After 10 p.m. over a hundred people were still continuing in prayer. This opened up a new phase of ministry for the church, not only to their own congregation, but to a steady flow of visitors from many other churches across the country which has continued ever since. Similarly, the South West London Vineyard has become a focal point for spreading the flame. In particular, Elli's address at Holy Trinity has probably become one of the most widely distributed tapes of recent years. To take just one example, Ian McFarlane played the tape to a meeting at Bookham Baptist Church. When it finished, they stood to wait upon the Lord and within seconds Ian fell to the floor. When he finally got back to his feet he realised that throughout the room people were being prayed for and were receiving from the Lord in power.

After these testimonies Joel and Lyndon needed much wisdom. Their delicate dilemma was how to facilitate ministry without imposing anything on those who were either unsure or even suspicious. With diplomatic flair their solution was a "comfort break". After an opportunity to queue for the toilets, the leaders were free either to go home or stay for further prayer. A few left but the vast majority stayed for what may well prove to have been the most significant prayer meeting in London for several decades.

The Spirit came upon the room in great waves of power. Brethren and Pentecostal, Anglicans, New Church and churches of every other stripe of evangelicalism were represented, and upon leader after leader the Spirit brought the awesome presence of God. It is always difficult to estimate such things, but it looked to me as if about two thirds of those present ended up on the floor at some stage. As Norman Moss moved around the room, Roger Forster caught his attention and asked for prayer. Norman promptly fell to his knees saying he would far rather Roger prayed for him. Roger began to pray but as he did so, the Spirit fell not on Norman but on Roger who stumbled forward into Norman's arms. Norman laid him out on the carpet and continued to pray for him. At one stage I was talking with Gerald Coates and R T Kendall. Gerald spoke about the immense impact this new wave was already having in Pioneer. R T stated his clear conviction that this was a genuine work of God and that the outward signs could be recognised as the hallmarks of previous times of refreshing and revival. Some leaders who had always been wary of charismatic renewal began to receive from the Spirit of God that morning.

From our own church, our director of evangelism was laid out on the floor, as was John Taylor, and also Bolt, the leader of our first church plant. It was early in the meeting that Bolt began to come under the impact of the Spirit. He felt so overwhelmed that he went outside for some fresh air. Returning to the meeting he realised that his symptoms were not due to indigestion but to the manifest presence of God. It was not long before he received in power. As for me, at first I felt a little detached from the ministry time, then the Spirit of God began to come upon me. It was like the rising tide, wave upon wave of the warmth of divine love. Nicky Gumbel prayed for me: "The Spirit of God is upon you, Rob." As I rested on the floor there was a twin focus to what God was doing in my life, pouring his love into my heart and anointing me with joy. Once again God was granting richly undeserved blessing. However, I could not help but notice how much less comfortable it is to fall on to an uncarpeted floor.

Once back on my feet, I joined the coffee queue. Even there we were not immune to the overwhelming presence of God. One man had just reached the front of the queue when, without warning or receiving prayer from anyone else, he collapsed to the floor and rested there in peace. Sipping my coffee I marvelled at the astonishing power of God breaking out upon London leaders. Not just in one church or stream, but right across the board, God was turning up the heat. I believe this amazing prayer meeting demonstrated that God is beginning to do things beyond anything seen in our land for generations. Oh Lord, that we might see you come in revival power!

When Lyndon Bowring pulled himself together sufficiently to set off for his next appointment he left me a message. "Isn't it wonderful! Tell Joel I am leaving him in full charge," he said, beaming. Joel Edwards, meanwhile, was lying flat on his back, his face tranquil, his attention fixed not on earthly things but on peace in the heavenlies.

On the night of the World Cup Final, 17 July, I was free from commitments at our church, so Claire and I decided to visit the South West London Vineyard in Putney. By now we had seen seven weeks of steady advancement in the refreshing. It was thrilling to see all that God was doing, but still we longed for much more, both for ourselves and for our church. Modern traffic in an ancient city spells frequent disaster, and when you live in inner London you get used to crawling along at less than ten miles per hour. Perhaps because the weather was so splendid, or possibly because day-trippers were hurrying home to see the match, on this particular evening the South Circular was almost stationary. It soon became apparent that reaching Putney at a decent hour was going to be impossible, and so we decided to divert to Wimbledon. Just as Holy Trinity, Brompton became a focal point north of the Thames, Queens Road, Wimbledon was taking on that role to the south. While their normal Sunday evening service continued, they had added a late night service running from 8.15 p.m. to around midnight.

We finally arrived in Wimbledon halfway through their first service. When they turned to prayer ministry we had not yet settled, so we decided to stay for the second meeting. Before it began, the room was already packed. Only one item was conspicuously absent: the chairs. Though some were left around the edge of the room for those who couldn't cope without, hundreds of people were standing or sitting on the carpet. The meeting was in five parts: a brief moment of worship; testimonies followed by further prayer to "light new fires"; a message from a visiting preacher; an explanation by Norman of what was going on, together with a clear explanation of the gospel and an invitation to become a Christian (about six responded the night we were present); and finally the time of prayer.

Claire is a much quieter person than me, with a gentle, sensitive nature. She wanted to give the Holy Spirit complete liberty in her life, but she feared embarrassment, thinking to herself: "I really hope the Spirit doesn't make me go over the top, laughing noisily." A member of the prayer team offered to pray for her, and almost immediately she began to laugh. Not a loud and raucous laugh, but quietly and yet from the heart. Then, as she continued to laugh, she also began to weep. God spoke to her, saying that the tears were expressing past hurts and disappointments but the laughter was a sign of a new day of blessing and joy. After laughing through the tears for a while, Claire began to feel overcome by the presence of God and fell to the floor, where the Lord continued to pour out an anointing of peace and joy.

When the prayer team turned to me there was no space left on the floor in our part of the room. Once we'd moved I fell to the floor under a fresh sense of the glory of God. This time I received a very distinct invitation: "Give me your heart." I realised afresh that in all my efforts to serve God zealously I so easily drift from the most important priority. God doesn't just want my service or my busy schedule of ministry, he wants my heart. God laid me out on the floor to arrest my attention. To get through to me about my own deepest needs he had to take me out of the action and so overwhelm me that I was in no position to do or say anything. I don't know how long I spent on the carpet, but this was a wonderful time of meeting with God and renewing my first love. When Claire came round and lifted her head the floor was littered with bodies. As she looked over in my direction she couldn't tell where I was: all she could see were row upon row of feet and she didn't know what the bottom of my trainers looked like! On the way home in the car we felt closer to one another than we had for years. It was a second honeymoon feeling. The reason was clear: the more intimate we become with the Lord, the greater our love for one another.

The next Tuesday I went back to Wimbledon for the leaders' meeting. I knew there was more I needed to receive. The meeting had begun with a handful of people, but now a couple of hundred had come together, some from a considerable distance. When my turn came for prayer I felt instantaneously drunk. I staggered a couple of steps, and fell to the ground. My hands began to twitch and shake, and then my whole body trembled as if I had been linked up to a high voltage cable. I heard the voice of God saying to me: "This is a revelation of my power. Not all of it, but as much as you can take right now." Even before I became a Christian I accepted the doctrine of God's omnipotence. I had no intellectual difficulty with the idea that God is all-powerful. But this was not a philosophical concept or a doctrinal formulation; this was a living encounter in the depths of my being. I was awestruck, filled with fear and trembling, before this personal demonstration of the formidable, incomparable power of God. Later I realised that this new encounter with God's power was in part a way of preparing me for our visit to Toronto a few days later.

Chapter 2

MEETING GOD IN POWER
– ENCOUNTERS IN THE BIBLE

Over the weeks since my conversation with Peter I had
not only met with God in the dramatic ways described in
the previous chapter, but I had also enjoyed less intense
times of refreshing when others in our church prayed for
me. But these weeks were not just about new encounters
with the Holy Spirit. It's difficult to know what to make
of unfamiliar spiritual experiences, without a framework of
similar encounters as points of reference, and so I sensed the
urgent need to provide such a context for myself and others.
As a result, a fire was ignited within me to scour the Bible
afresh and devour every book on revival that I could lay my
hands on. In this chapter we will take a fresh look at a biblical
perspective on meeting God in power.

Saul overcome
No Old Testament encounters with the Spirit of God are
more astonishing than those of King Saul. Before he was
made king, Saul had his first power encounter. In preparation, Saul received very exact and detailed words of
knowledge from Samuel, culminating with the promise that
he would meet a group of prophets and then his life would
be changed. These prophets were of a different type to the
later "writing prophets", like Isaiah and Jeremiah. We have
no record of their prophecies, though they were plainly
renowned for their prophetic fluency. We know little about
them personally except that they travelled around together,
taking their music with them, praising God and declaring

prophecies whenever the Spirit came upon them. They were, if you like, a kind of Jewish charismatic gypsy band.

> As you approach the town, you will meet a procession of prophets coming down from the high place with lyres, tambourines, flutes and harps being played before them, and they will be prophesying. The Spirit of the LORD will come upon you in power, and you will prophesy with them; and you will be changed into a different person.
>
> (1 Sam 10:5–6)

What do we make of this curious incident? While God is quite capable of touching someone directly, without any human intermediary, it seems he often prefers to use anointed individuals as channels of his power. To be sure, Saul did receive from God possibly without even knowing it, in a direct but hidden touch, for prior to his meeting with the prophets we are told that God changed Saul's heart (1 Sam 10:9). Here is God stepping in to begin a work of transformation beyond Saul's own capacities. The full measure of blessing was yet to come, but at this stage Saul became ready and willing to receive. He became prepared to go in humility to receive from those who already knew the working of the Spirit's power. While Saul made a choice to meet up with the prophets, it seems he had no real choice about the impact of that encounter on his life. So powerfully was the Spirit of God present among them that Saul quickly came under the influence and began to prophesy, just as Samuel had foretold.

There were three results of the Spirit of God coming in power. Firstly, there was an immediate outward manifestation – Saul prophesied. Secondly there was an inner transformation. Samuel had promised not merely that Saul would have a supernatural experience, but that he would be radically transformed on the inside. Presumably God could have completed this inner change without any dramatic experiences and manifestations, but in Saul's case God chose to work with this spectacular external display of unprecedented prophesying. The third result was that Saul could return to his everyday life and work with a new confidence in the presence and help of God. As Samuel expressed it, "Once these signs are fulfilled, do whatever your hand finds to do, for God is with you" (1 Sam 10:7). These three phases are very striking, because they are paralleled in many testimonies today: first a power encounter accompanied by outward manifestations, then inner change, followed by a new sense of God's daily presence.

The reaction of others to Saul's empowerment and subsequent appointment as king is divided. While some are inspired by the evidence of God's hand upon his life, others despise him and can see no reason to believe in him (1 Sam 10:27). Whenever God moves in power, we always face a critical choice: do we accept or reject what we see? Since some refused to see the hand of God even in the miracles of Jesus, it should hardly surprise us that some sneer and scoff when the Spirit is poured out today.

Saul's time as king is ultimately disastrous as he sinks from disregarding Samuel to eventually plotting to kill David, his appointed successor. His life therefore stands as a stark reminder that past blessing is no guarantee against future failure. It is vital that we heed this warning for our own lives, so that we never try to live off the capital of past blessings whilst drifting ever farther from God in the present.

The Holy Spirit's second power encounter with Saul is even more awesome than the first (1 Sam 19). Despite giving an oath to his son Jonathan that David will not be put to death, Saul decides he can tolerate David's existence no more and so instructs soldiers to murder him. David manages to escape the first assault and flees to Samuel for help at a place called Naioth at Ramah. Unfortunately, Saul discovers his whereabouts and once again sends soldiers to kill him.

When the soldiers arrive at Ramah, they come across Samuel surrounded by a band of prophets who are prophesying. Note that the charismatic gypsies have turned up again. We are not told explicitly but it seems reasonable to assume that Samuel had requested their help to protect David, not by taking up arms but as a spiritual force. Clearly when these men were prophesying together under the manifest presence of God, a spiritual authority was released that was greater than the might of the soldiers. Swords and plans to kill count for nothing compared with the forcefulness of the Spirit of God. So powerful is the presence of God that the Spirit promptly comes upon the soldiers. Utterly disarmed, they are unable to do anything except prophesy too, quite incapable of carrying out their king's orders. Saul sends a second squad, and then a third, but the Spirit comes in power upon them, so they too end up prophesying.

No doubt exasperated at his crack troops' inability to carry out a simple execution, Saul finally decides to complete the task himself. However, when he drew near to the place, "the Spirit of God came even upon him," with the result that he began to walk along the road prophesying. When he came into Samuel's presence he did more than prophesy, for he stripped off his robes and lay down naked, remaining like that for a day and a night.

What can we make of this deeply disturbing power encounter? Without warning, Saul's own murderous intentions were overcome. His rational faculties were overpowered. In stripping off his clothes and lying down naked he was surely behaving as if drunk or mad. It seems clear that he was completely mastered and even humiliated by the Spirit of God. What we see here is the sheer forcefulness of the coming of the Spirit. Although the Spirit came upon Saul once to bless and once to condemn, on both occasions he was quite overwhelmed by the manifest presence of the living God.

Elders overcome

What of others who were spontaneously touched by God? In Numbers 11, the Israelites encounter both judgment and blessing. As to judgment, when the people begin to complain once more about their hardships, fire from heaven breaks out around the edge of the camp and a number are consumed. Only when Moses prays for mercy does the fire die down (Num 11:1–3). Later in the chapter Moses calls seventy elders to stand with him as he prays. The cloud of divine glory comes upon Moses and the Lord takes a portion of the Spirit from the great leader of Israel and causes the same Spirit to rest upon the elders. As the Spirit comes upon them, the elders prophesy. This is a unique experience, for they never prophesy again. Here again we see the pattern of the manifest presence of God being passed from person to person, accompanied by the manifestation of prophecy.

Still more striking is the experience of Eldad and Medad. Although listed among the elders, for some reason they failed to go out to the tent with the others. When the Spirit came upon the elders around Moses, these two had a divine visitation simultaneously, with the result that they prophesied too. There's no suggestion that they were praying and seeking God. The implication seems to be the reverse, since they failed even to turn up at the prayer meeting. But God in his sovereign authority determined to manifest his presence upon every elder without exception, and so, without warning, he came upon Eldad and Medad in the camp. Here we see that when God is pouring out his Spirit in power, even those who are not actively seeking God may suddenly be overcome by his manifest presence. Once again the prophecy itself is not recorded. This is not prophecy with the authoritative status of Scripture. Instead it seems to be a kind of by-product or visual aid, the immediate evidence of a power encounter with the living God.

Priests overcome
In the days of Solomon, the external manifestation when God came in power was not a matter of doing something new but rather being prevented from doing something familiar. Solomon had spent a full seven years building the temple, although the historian who wrote the book of Kings could not help but observe regretfully that he took up to thirteen years to build his own palace. This temple was the pride of Israel, constructed of the finest materials in the hands of the most able craftsmen and adorned by renowned artists from around the Middle East. When the Ark of the covenant, dating back to the days of Moses, was brought into its new

resting place, a great festival of praise had been planned. The priests were gathered in their splendid robes. The Levites who were musicians assembled together in white linen, holding their cymbals, harps and lyres. The sound of 120 trumpets rang out as the singers began their first song of praise: "He is good; his love endures for ever."

No doubt many pieces of inspirational music had been prepared for such an historic day, complete with grand processions around the temple. But in an instant everything ground to a halt. The reason was simple: God stepped in. The cloud of the glory of the Lord came down and completely filled the temple. So awesome, so immediate was the presence of the Lord that everything planned was abandoned: "the priests could not perform their service because of the cloud" (1 Kgs 8:6–11; 2 Chr 5:11–14). Later that day, when Solomon had declared his prayer of dedication, the divine presence was manifest anew. Fire from heaven came down to consume the burnt offering and once more "the glory of the Lord filled the temple" (2 Chr 7:1). The divine presence was again disruptive, for again the priests were unable to enter the temple to perform their duties. The presence of the glory of the Lord was too much to bear.

Prophet overcome
Isaiah's personal encounter with the glory of the Lord was also in the temple (Isa 6:1–10). So transcendent, so beyond human comprehension or language is the holiness and glory of the Lord that Isaiah describes the surrounding seraphs more fully than the divine majesty they adore. If the first impact of Isaiah's encounter is awesome, it becomes increasingly terrifying. First the very building seems to shake, and then the temple fills with smoke. While the smoke takes us back to the shekinah cloud of glory, the shaking of the room takes us forward to Acts 4, where Luke records that the divine presence is manifested in the building being shaken (Acts 4:31).

Isaiah's reaction to this revelation of breathtaking power and holiness is outright fear. He believes he is on the brink of death, for God's splendour exposes not only the moral impurity of Israel, but also Isaiah's own. Only by the mercy of God can Isaiah be freed from guilt and sin. We cannot tell whether the presence was immediately disruptive on this occasion, since Isaiah does not explain what he was originally planning to do in the temple that day. He may have been officiating, but that remains unclear. What we do know is that the consequences were disruptive, because at the end of this encounter Isaiah receives his commission to be a prophet, and so his life will never be the same again.

There is much that we can learn from Isaiah. He cannot bring about the revelation of the divine presence; only God can do this. He cannot earn forgiveness; he can only throw himself on the mercy of God. Personal revival, which is surely what Isaiah experienced, is not something we can work up and complete for ourselves. It is only possible thanks to the graciousness of God.

A city overcome
In the days of Nehemiah and Ezra, after the walls of Jerusalem had been rebuilt, the people gathered to hear Ezra read from the Law of Moses. The day began with worship; the people lifted their hands, cried out in prayer and then bowed down to worship the Lord with their faces to the ground. The Law was read from daybreak until noon, and so moved were the people that Nehemiah records that as they listened to the Law being declared once more, they all began to weep (Neh 8). These events represent a decisive turning point for ancient Israel, nothing less than a revival of true religion in Jerusalem. It was one thing to rebuild the city, another to be rebuilt spiritually by God. As the Word of God is faithfully declared, God works in unexpected power among the people, way beyond and even contrary to the expectations of their leaders. Ezra and Nehemiah clearly intended the reading of the law to be a joyous occasion, because they keep telling the people not to mourn, weep or grieve. But where the Spirit of God brings conviction of sin, no palliative measures can soothe the conscience. The people needed genuine, heartfelt repentance and nothing less. A few

weeks later they met again, fasting and wearing sackcloth, with dust on their heads. In the meantime they had sorted their lives out in practical repentance and now they engaged in public confession of sin (Neh 9).

In due course, the people were able to arrive at the expressions of joy which the leaders had promoted prematurely. Tears of repentance turned to songs and shouts of joy with such volume that, as Nehemiah records, "The sound of rejoicing in Jerusalem could be heard far away" (Neh 12:43). This remarkable episode marks the most incisive period of revival in the Old Testament. As the Holy Spirit moves in unexpected power upon the people, the leaders suddenly become observers of a mighty work of God. Ezra and Nehemiah have the privilege of witnessing profound conviction of sin with much weeping, genuine and deep repentance, and finally the reverberating sound of heartfelt rejoicing. What's more this wonderful revival embraced not just a few but the vast majority of the inhabitants of the city.

Seeking more

So far we have considered examples of those who met with God in power more or less unexpectedly. We turn now to two examples of those who actively sought to know more of God and his ways: Moses and Gideon.

Moses had remarkable power encounters with the living God, from the moment he faced the burning bush. But still he longs for more, and so he pleads that he might be taught the ways of God more fully (Exod 33–4). His motives are twofold: to truly know God, and for God to hold him in favour. God's immediate response is to promise that his manifest presence will continue to be with Moses. Moses gladly receives the promise, declaring that the divine presence will distinguish the Israelites from all other peoples and demonstrate to others that God's pleasure rests upon his chosen people. But still he asks for more: "Show me your glory." What follows is an attempt to describe the inexpressible. Words strain at the limits of both language and the rational mind to describe the intensity and drama of Moses's encounter with God. This is no theoretical concept or doctrine of God. This is God's manifest presence in glory.

The response Moses receives is that God will provide both a revelation of his glory and yet protection:

> I will cause all my goodness to pass in front of you, and I will proclaim my name, the LORD, in your presence . . . When my glory passes by, I will . . . cover you with my hand until I have passed by. Then I will remove my hand . . . my face must not be seen.
>
> (Exod 33:19–23)

God will not reveal more of his awesome glory than Moses can handle. What's more, while this begins the period of Moses's most intense and direct encounters with God, where there is revelation, there is also mystery. Moses sees God's glory but sees it obliquely; the infinite majesty of God can only be grasped partially by the finite mind.

As we might expect, the first thing this experience inspires is worship, but when Moses comes back down the mountain, the people's astonishment reveals a side-effect to which he had previously been oblivious: his face was radiant with the afterglow of God's glorious presence. So intense is this physical manifestation that the people are filled with fear and refuse to come near him. Eventually Moses realises that the only solution is to wear a veil to hide the dazzling brightness. Just as had been promised, the Lord's manifest presence continues to be available to Moses, and so when Moses prays he removes the veil, but before the people Moses is obliged to hide his face. Clearly this was a continuing experience, but we are not told for how long Moses had to wear a veil in this way. This dazzling side-effect of the divine presence is found with even greater intensity at Jesus's transfiguration, where his "face shone like the sun, and his clothes became as white as the light" (Matt 17:2).

Turning to Gideon, there is a longing at the heart of his life that is echoed in every generation of Christians who have prayed earnestly for revival. He longs for a renewed outpouring of God's power on the face of the earth: "Where are all his wonders that our fathers told us about . . .?" (Judg 6:13). Without realising it, Gideon is already seeing the beginning of that renewal in his own day, for his conversation is with none other than the angel of the Lord. Almost immediately Gideon receives a promise and a manifestation familiar from the days of Moses – the promise of divine presence (Judg 6:16) and then an encounter with heavenly fire (Judg 6:21). As usually proves necessary, God has to speak peace upon Gideon, who is terrified by the revelation (Judg 6:22–3). Then he is commanded to destroy his father's equipment for idol worship (Judg 6:25–6). Once again a revelation of God leads to a call for purification from sin and a restoration of right living.

The second stage of Gideon's story begins with the miracles of the fleece, wet when the ground was dry, then dry when the ground was wet, just as he had requested (Judg 6:36–40). Thereafter, the "wonders that our fathers told us about" are truly restored in the miraculous victory of the Midianites, following the reduction of Gideon's army from 32,000 to 300, with the express intention that God alone should receive all glory for the triumphant rout (Judg 7). Once again we see the manifest presence of God leading to behaviour that is strange to say the least by any normal standards. To prune an army by over ninety-nine per cent is nothing less than absurd. To march around the enemy camp with trumpets and jars is hardly a conventional military strategy. God's instructions not only require such an unconventional approach, but he is also at work in the enemy camp. First he sends a dream to one of the Midianites which is interpreted to signify that Midianite destruction is at hand, and then he causes the enemy soldiers to strike at one another in terror and confusion.

Gideon rejoices to see the renewal of God's works of power for which he had longed. It would have been fatuous for him to try to organise such a renewal; all he could do was pray. But when God broke out in power we see a familiar pattern: supernatural encounters that bring fear; a call to radical repentance; bizarre behaviour that makes no sense at all according to normal human wisdom and conventions. When Gideon's heartfelt prayer is echoed in our generation, it should come as no surprise if our experiences are similarly powerful, life-changing and bizarre.

The manifest presence

What then are the implications of these Old Testament encounters with God? Firstly a doctrine of God's omni-presence is inadequate to account for such moments. To be sure, God is unrestricted by time and space, as Psalm 139 celebrates so eloquently. But in each of these encounters we find something more than God's omnipresence, namely God's manifest presence, specific and unmistakable. Person after person in the Old Testament is caught up in these revelatory encounters, more real, immediate and direct than our ordinary sense impressions.

This manifest presence can only be described as over-whelming, since it generally leads to fear of the Lord, manifestations previously unseen and the cessation of pre-vious patterns of behaviour, whether through repentance or because of an awed stillness. What's more, this presence is almost invasive: although it can be prayed for, it cannot be manufactured or worked up by human effort, by devised methods or a deliberate stirring of emotions. This is a coming of God in power and all that people can do is to receive with awe.

As I studied afresh these Old Testament events of meeting God in power, I realised that a favourite English tradition was being blown out of the water. I remember being told as a young Christian that the Holy Spirit is a "gentleman", who always visits the church in a gentle, courteous and discreet manner, never imposing anything upon us that we would find disturbing and strange. Biblical experiences of God's manifest presence make complete garbage of such complacency. Of course God is sensitive to what we can take as individuals, but this teaching that God always comes to us as a gentleman is palpable nonsense. It is not biblical Christianity; it is deceptive idolatry. As a result of such conditioning, if we see manifestations that are "ungentlemanly" our knee-jerk reflex is to dismiss them: "That cannot possibly be of God." We have caged the divine, remaking God in our own image and redefining acceptable behaviour on God's part within our own comfort zones. Any teaching or attitude that excludes the overwhelming, manifest presence of God will be able neither to expect nor to accept times of refreshing and revival. Quite simply, it is above all in revival that people come face to face with the wonderful yet always awesome power of the manifest presence of God.

New Testament manifestations

Turning to the New Testament, meeting God in power takes on a new intensity, first in the healings and miracles of Jesus, when people are confronted directly and repeatedly with the inbreaking of the Kingdom of God, and then in the early church. Just as Jesus had promised, the first Christians were "clothed with power from on high" (Luke 24:49). At the day of Pentecost the sound of a wind filling the room and the sight of flames resting upon each person were the first signs of God's manifest presence. At once they knew they were baptised with the Spirit of God and this inner reality was accompanied by the outward manifestations of speaking in tongues and worship. Only when the Spirit came did they see a great harvest of souls, with 3,000 professing faith that day.

The Spirit didn't merely bring the presence of God on the day of Pentecost and then promptly recede from the Church. When Luke describes the Church in Jerusalem at the end of Acts 2, he states that two key evidences of the manifest presence continued among them: the apostles continued to do many wonders and miraculous signs, and everyone was filled with awe (Acts 2:43). Why the awe? Because God was unmistakably present in power. How often has church life declined into a religious routine, where power and awe have been replaced with predictability and boredom!

In Acts 4, the Spirit was again poured out upon the Jerusalem Church, as a direct result of their ardent and urgent prayers for help. As usual there was a sign of the coming of God, for on this occasion the building seemed to shake around them. Once more Luke reports that they were filled with the Spirit, and this time the outward sign was that they spoke the word of God boldly. The phrase is oblique; it could mean witness, it could mean prophecy, and it presumably may also indicate another fervent outbreak of tongues. The one thing that is absolutely clear is that, having been filled at Pentecost, further fillings were extremely welcome and the believers received this fresh wave of the Spirit with grateful hearts. Later in the chapter, Luke underlines the continued anointing upon the Church: "With great power the apostles continued to testify to the resurrection of the Lord Jesus, and much grace was upon them all" (Acts 4:33). There was both a sustained empowering and also the opportunity for further power encounters with the manifest presence of God.

In Acts 10, Cornelius and his household receive the Holy Spirit during Peter's preaching. This is the first example of a sermon being interrupted in revival by a mighty outpouring of the Spirit of God. If we have been conditioned to suppose that every sermon is like a lecture, with no interruption permissible until the last sentence has been delivered, we may need to think again. When the Church is in revival, so great is the response to the preached word that sometimes the end of the sermon is never reached. As Luke describes it, "the Holy Spirit came on all who heard the message" (Acts 10:44), with the immediate result that, while Peter is still preaching, Cornelius and the others begin praising God in tongues. Instead of rebuking them for rudely interrupting him or for a lack of "decency and order", Peter has the wisdom to abandon the sermon and baptise the new converts. His reason is plain: "They have received the Holy Spirit just as we have" (Acts 10:47).

Our final example from Acts is the conversion of Paul (Acts 9). Here is a man who encounters the manifest presence of God, not when he is praying ardently, nor when someone is preaching the gospel, but when he is travelling from Jerusalem to Damascus to persecute Christians. Again there is a sign of God's coming, this time a bright light flashing around him. As with many who meet with God in power, Saul's involuntary reaction is to fall to the ground. While he rests there he hears a voice from heaven, revealing Christ's true glory and calling him to repentance. As a prophetic sign of his former spiritual blindness, Saul is made temporarily blind; then he is sent to Damascus where he fasts for three days, awaiting further instructions. Eventually a rather reluctant Ananias visits him, having received direct instructions from God. When Ananias prays for Saul, Saul is filled with the Spirit, his sight is restored, and then he is baptised in water.

What do we make of such a dramatic conversion, with visions and voices, a dazzling light and falling down, sudden blindness and healing? When the Spirit of God is being poured out abundantly, some who are unbelievers or even virulent opponents of Christ meet with God in such power that they are stopped in their tracks, seized by the truths of judgment and grace, with the result that their lives are utterly and spontaneously re-directed. This is not a work of the Church in our weakness, nor the fruit of organised evangelism. This is the work of God in revival power.

It's quite impossible to understand the spiritual dynamic of the early church in terms of normal church life today. To be sure, they were a church of sinners just like us, with mixed motives, secret sins and difficult relationships. But they also knew something more. They were not simply Bible-believing Christians, nor merely charismatics in renewal. The only adequate explanation of the amazing effectiveness with which God was working through the first Christians is this: the early church was a church in revival. Of course, strictly speaking the first Christians could not be revived; they had entered into abundant spiritual life for the first time and as yet there had been no decline. But if we want to define revival we can do no better than look at the book of Acts: here, for the first time, the Spirit of God was poured out upon the Church in what we have since come to know as revival power.

Apostolic expectations

Paul's letters underline the vital importance of knowing the manifest presence of God. To the Thessalonians he describes his own preaching ministry: "Our gospel came to you not simply with words, but also with power, with the Holy Spirit and deep conviction" (1 Thess 1:5). Similarly to the Corinthians he stresses the absolute priority of a living encounter with the power of the Holy Spirit: "My message and my preaching were not with wise and persuasive words, but with a demonstration of the Spirit's power" (1 Cor 2:4). How often has the Church exchanged power for eloquence and learning, producing golden-tongued theorists who are spiritually powerless? A young ministerial student was being commended to an old Welsh preacher for his fine intellect and many gifts. "All very well," the old man said, "but can he pray down the Holy Spirit upon a congregation?" For Paul the crucial issue was the appropriate basis for faith. He wanted no one's profession of faith to depend on human wisdom or persuasiveness. He was convinced that true faith needed to rest on a "demonstration of the Spirit's power". Small wonder that we have lost the Apostolic effectiveness, when we have neglected the Apostolic priorities.

Paul by no means restricted this emphasis to his own preaching ministry. He described to the Corinthians what he expected to be the essential pattern of their regular meetings: "When you are assembled in the name of our Lord Jesus . . . and the power of our Lord Jesus is present" (1 Cor 5:4). In short, orthodox beliefs are not enough, nor are declarations *about* the power of God. Paul expects the Corinthians to know more than the doctrines of saving truth. He expects them to have a living encounter with God when they meet together. Just as we are confident in the availability of running water or electricity, Paul was confident that the early churches would know and experience the availability of genuine Holy Spirit power.

The powerful presence of the Holy Spirit yokes earth and heaven, the finite and the infinite, the present and the future. In the coming of Jesus, his teaching and miracles, his death and resurrection, the manifest presence of God makes its most decisive impact upon this world. Jesus's favourite phrase, the Kingdom of God, speaks of the presence of the future, the rule of heaven beginning to break through on the face of the earth. This same dynamic of present fulfilment combined with future expectation is found in several Pauline metaphors for the Holy Spirit. He is the firstfruit, presently enjoyed and promising the full harvest to come (Rom 8:23). He is the seal of new ownership, set upon those for whom the master will later return (2 Cor 1:22; Eph 1:13). He is the downpayment or deposit, guaranteeing future payment in full (2 Cor 1:22). (The word used here, *arrabon*, has taken on in modern Greek the meaning of an engagement ring, which underlines this sense of present gift and future expectancy.) All these metaphors illumine the same dynamic interface: whenever the Spirit is poured out freely, we discover the presence of the future. With overflowing joy we can delight in the manifest presence of God by his Spirit, knowing that our personal experiences really have become a wonderful foretaste of heaven.

In the light of the experiences and expectations of the first Christians, we can draw some crucial conclusions not only about meeting God in power but also about revival.

* Revival is an outpouring of the Spirit of God.
* Revival is a work of God in power.
* The Church in the New Testament, warts and all, is a church in revival.
* When the Church enters revival, we experience days of heaven on earth.
* All subsequent revivals entail nothing less than a return to something of the spiritual vitality of the early church.

Chapter 3

THE GREAT AWAKENING

When the Spirit has begun to be poured out upon us in greater measure than for many decades, at a time when we are seeing an increase not only in awareness of God but also of physical manifestations, it makes sense to look again at periods of revival. What can we learn from the work of the Holy Spirit in previous generations? In this chapter I will concentrate upon the period of the Great Awakening in the United States and Britain, quoting frequently from those directly involved so that we can hear from them afresh in our day.

The Great Awakening, centred on the year 1740, saw a momentous surge in conversions and spiritual vitality across the English-speaking world. Estimates for the number of new converts in the American colonies alone vary from 25,000 to 50,000 and many more Christians had their faith re-invigorated. William Cooper of Boston observed, in 1741, what he termed the uniformity of the work:

> By the accounts I have received in letters, and conversations with ministers and others, who live in different parts of the land where this work is going on, it is the same work that is carried on in one place and another: the method of the Spirit's operation on the minds of the people is the same . . . and the particular appearances with which this work is attended, that have not been so common at other times, are also much the same. (J Edwards, *Distinguishing Marks*, p. 81)

As Cooper assessed this remarkable new outpouring of the Spirit of God, he declared with understandable excitement and wonder: "The apostolical times seem to have returned upon us; such a display has there been of the power and grace of the divine Spirit in the assemblies of his people, and such testimonies has he given to the word of the Gospel" (J Edwards, *Distinguishing Marks*, p. 77).

Powerful conversions

The leaders of revivals are characterised by intense personal encounters with God, both in their conversions and in moments of powerful anointing for public ministry. For Charles and John Wesley, it was after their ordinations and a period of failed service as missionaries that they were finally born again. Charles was the first. In May 1738 he was sick and often in bed, but at the same time was actively seeking living faith in Christ. On Pentecost Sunday, 21 May, a recent convert burst for a brief moment into the room when he was resting and cried out, "In the name of Jesus of Nazareth, arise, believe, and thou shalt be healed of all thy infirmities!" Later, while he was still trying to find who had intervened so dramatically, he experienced a physical and spiritual reaction: "I felt in the meantime a strange palpitation of heart. I said, yet feared to say, 'I believe, I believe!'" Although the following hours and days were frequently filled with doubts and fears, Charles had nonetheless found a new centre in his relationship with Christ: "I now found myself at peace with God, and rejoiced in the hope of loving Christ."

By no means all Charles's friends were pleased with his new-found faith. One who called to see him feared he was going mad. Mockingly he said he expected to see rays of light about Charles's head. He urged Charles to flee London, for the sake of his sanity and religious well-being, but he failed to win Charles over, who ends the episode in his journal with the words, "In despair of me, he left."

John Wesley had been a dedicated participant in "The

Holy Club" while at Oxford, a small group devoted to self-sacrifice in the service of God. They were also nicknamed "Bible Moths", "Bible Bigots", "Sacramentarians" and "Methodists". Despite his best efforts, both there and in Georgia, he made no real headway in his faith: "In this refined way of trusting to my own works and my own righteousness . . . I dragged on heavily, finding no comfort or help in it." When he returned to England at the end of his missionary service he wrote in his journal:

> I want that faith which none can have without knowing that he has it . . . He is freed from fear, having peace with God through Christ, and rejoicing in the hope of the glory of God, and he is freed from doubt, having the love of God shed abroad in his heart through the Holy Ghost which is given him, the Spirit himself bearing witness with his spirit that he is a child of God. (J Wesley, *Journal*, 1 February 1738)

Back in London, John met a Moravian called Peter Böhler, with whom he entered into theological dispute. Despite intellectual resistance, in his heart John capitulated, observing: "If, then, there was no faith without this sense of forgiveness, all my pretensions to faith fell at once." The next day they met again and the Moravian brought with him three converts, who all testified to the experience of a "true, living faith in Christ". John now began to seek this faith, renouncing "all dependence, in whole or in part, upon my own works or righteousness, on which from my youth I had really grounded my hope of salvation, though I did not know it".

Finally, on the evening of Wednesday, 24 May 1738, he attended a meeting in Aldersgate Street and while someone read from Luther's preface to the Epistle to the Romans, he received his salvation:

> About a quarter before nine, while he was describing the change which God works in the heart through faith in Christ, I felt my heart strangely warmed. I felt I did trust

in Christ, Christ alone, for salvation, and an assurance was given me that He had taken away my sins, even mine, and saved me from the law of sin and death.

While John received peace with God and new victory over sin, joy seemed absent. On reflection he concluded: "As far as the transports of joy usually attending the beginning of it, especially in those who have mourned deeply, God sometimes gives and sometimes withholds them, according to the counsels of his own will."

George Whitefield also became a member of The Holy Club, striving to win the favour of God. When reading Henry Scougal's book, *The Life of God in the Soul of Man*, his understanding of Christian faith was revolutionised: "God showed me that I must be born again, or be damned! I learned that a man may go to church, say his prayer, receive the sacrament, and yet not be a Christian" (quoted in Dallimore, *George Whitefield*, p. 18). In the coming weeks he became desperate, fearing that he was eternally lost:

My comforts were soon withdrawn, and a horrible fearfulness and dread permitted to overwhelm my soul. One morning in particular . . . I felt an unusual impression and weight upon my breast, attended with inward darkness . . . Whole days and weeks have I spent in lying prostrate on the ground. (Quoted in Dallimore, *George Whitefield*, p. 19)

From autumn 1734 to spring 1735 he became more desperate until at last he experienced saving faith:

God was pleased to remove the heavy load, to enable me to lay hold on his dear Son by a living faith, and by giving me the spirit of adoption, to seal me, even to the day of everlasting redemption. O! With what joy – joy unspeakable – even joy that was full of and big with glory, was my soul filled, when the weight of sin went off, and an abiding sense of the pardoning love of God . . . broke in upon my disconsolate soul! Surely it was . . . a day to be had in everlasting remembrance! My joys were like a spring tide, and overflowed the banks. (Quoted in Dallimore, *George Whitefield*, p. 21)

Howel Harris, who became a great leader of the revival in Wales, had a similarly overwhelming encounter with God on 18 June that same summer, 1735:

I felt suddenly my heart melting within me, like wax before the fire, with love to God my Saviour. I felt not only love and peace, but also a *longing* to be dissolved and to be with Christ; and there was a cry in my inmost soul, with which I was totally unacquainted before, it was this – *Abba, Father*; *Abba, Father*! I could not help calling God *my* Father; I knew that I was his child, and that he loved me; my soul being filled and satiated, crying, "It is enough – I am satisfied; give me strength, and I will follow thee through fire and water." I could now say that I was happy indeed. There was in me "a well of water springing up into everlasting life"; yea, "the love of God was shed abroad in my heart by the Holy Ghost". (Quoted in Evans, *The Welsh Revival of 1904* p. 67)

Later revivalists enjoyed similarly intense encounters with the manifest presence of God. In the early nineteenth century Charles Finney's future ministry was sealed by fire from on high:

Without any expectation of it, without ever having the thought in my mind that there was any such thing for me, without any memory of ever hearing the thing mentioned by any person in the world, the Holy Spirit descended upon me in a manner that seemed to go through me, body and soul. I could feel the impression, like a wave of electricity, going through me and through me. Indeed it seemed to come in waves of liquid love, for I could not express it in any other way. It seemed like the very breath of God. I can remember distinctly that it seemed to fan me, like immense wings.

No words can express the wonderful love that was shed abroad in my heart. I wept aloud with joy and love. I literally bellowed out the unspeakable overflow of my heart. These waves came over me, and over me, and over me, one after the other, until I remember crying out, "I shall die if these waves continue to pass over me." I said, "Lord, I cannot bear any more," yet I had no fear of death. (Finney, *Autobiography*, pp. 21–2)

Some fifty years later, in 1871, D L Moody had an overwhelming encounter with God that empowered his future ministry as an international evangelist. He had been converted during a revival in Boston on Sunday, 22 April 1855, at which time he experienced abundant joy:

I thought the old sun shone a good deal brighter than it ever had before – I thought that it was just smiling upon me; and as I walked out upon Boston common and heard the birds singing in the trees, I thought they were all singing a song for me . . . It seemed to me that I was in love with all creation. I had not a bitter feeling against any man, and I was ready to take all men to my heart.

Later, Moody wrestled with God for personal spiritual revival, a personal Pentecost. Suddenly one day, as he walked down Fifth Avenue or Broadway – afterwards he could never remember which – the presence of God came overwhelmingly upon him. He hurried to the nearby house of a friend and urgently requested a room where he could be on his own. As the room blazed with the presence of God he fell to the floor, resting in the presence of God. As for others before and since, the impact of God's manifest presence was so powerful that he thought he might die: "I can only say that God revealed himself to me, and I had such an experience of his love that I had to ask him to stay his hand." Before he had been striving for God, but now the life of God flowed through him with new liberty: "I was all the time tugging and carrying water. But now I have a river that carries me."

Our third and final example of a later revival leader

receiving power from on high is Evan Roberts, from the Welsh Revival of 1904.

> One Friday night last spring, when praying by my bedside before retiring, I was taken up to a great expanse – without time and space. It was communion with God. Before this I had a far-off God. I was frightened that night, but never since. So great was my shivering that I rocked the bed, and my brother, being awakened, took hold of me thinking I was ill. After that experience I was wakened every night a little after one o'clock. This was most strange, for through the years I slept like a rock, and no disturbance in my room would awaken me. From that hour I was taken up into the divine fellowship for about four hours. What it was I cannot tell you, except that it was divine. About five o'clock I was again allowed to sleep on till about nine. At this time I was again taken up into the same experience as in the earlier hours of the morning until about twelve or one o'clock . . . This went on for about three months. (Quoted in Evans, *The Welsh Revival of 1904*, pp. 65–6)

Although conversion experiences rightly and necessarily concentrate on the saving power of the cross of Christ, we also note the frequent return to the following Scriptures to describe and explain these personal preparations for revival:

> Whoever believes in me, as the Scripture has said, streams of living water will flow from within him.
>
>   (John 7:38)

> And hope does not disappoint us, because God has poured out his love into our hearts by the Holy Spirit, whom he has given us.
>
>   (Rom 5:5)

> For you did not receive a spirit that makes you a slave again to fear, but you received the Spirit of sonship. And by him we cry, "*Abba*, Father." The Spirit himself testifies with our spirit that we are God's children.
>
>   (Rom 8:15–16)

Though you have not seen him, you love him; and even
though you do not see him now, you believe in him and
are filled with an inexpressible and glorious joy.

(1 Pet 1:8)

Manifestations

The Great Awakening is primarily about vast numbers
coming to saving faith in Christ. The biblical doctrines of
grace that had been recovered at the Reformation were
pressed home first upon the lives of these leaders and then
upon the thousands who gathered to hear them preach. But
revival is always about more than gifted evangelists. Frequent
in the contemporary descriptions of amazing events are
accounts of God coming upon meetings in power. Jonathan
Edwards spoke often about "outpourings of the Spirit" while
Whitefield wrote of "demonstrations of the Spirit" and "the
power of God so obviously among us". He also described
the Spirit "coming into the congregation like a mighty
rushing wind, carrying all before it" (Whitefield, *Journals*,
6 June 1740).

Revival is not simply organised evangelism; it is a mighty
visitation of the Spirit of God. And where God comes
powerfully among his people there are always physical signs
of his presence. As you read the following descriptions of
manifestations you will discover that such things are nothing
new, no strange innovation or excess of the late twentieth
century. Though these things are by no means the most
important aspect of revival, where there is revival, and the
Spirit is poured out in power, similar strange and strong
manifestations can be expected.

One Presbyterian minister in New Londonderry, Samuel
Blair, wrote in 1744 this summary of the phenomena seen
in his church in revival:

Our Sabbath assemblies soon became vastly large; many
people from almost all parts around inclining very much
to come where there was such appearance of the divine

power and presence. I think there was scarcely a sermon or lecture preached here through the whole summer, but there were manifest evidences of impressions on the hearers; and many times the impressions were very great and general. Several would be overcome and fainting; others deeply sobbing, hardly able to contain; others crying in a most dolorous manner; many others more silently weeping; and a solemn concern appearing in the countenances of many others. And sometimes the soul exercise of some (though comparatively but few) would so far affect their bodies as to occasion some strange unusual bodily motions. (Quoted in Tracy, *The Great Awakening*, p. 28)

Jonathan Edwards' summary list was similar: "tears, trembling, groans, loud outcries, agonies of body, or the failing of bodily strength" (J Edwards, *Distinguishing Marks*, p. 91).

Weeping
George Whitefield and John Wesley may have seen more weeping than any other preachers in Christian history. Wesley often described congregations "melted in tears". On 27 November 1739 Whitefield preached for nearly two hours, "with such demonstration of the Spirit that great numbers continued weeping for a considerable time". The following May his plans to preach were overcome by great weeping, which in turn led to cries of anguish, deep and public repentance, and even some people shaking as if epileptic:

As soon as I entered the room and heard them singing, my soul was delighted. When the hymn was over I desired to pray before I began to converse; but my soul was so carried out that I had no time to talk at all. A wonderful power was in the room and with one accord they began to cry out and weep most bitterly for half an hour. They seemed to be under the strongest convictions, and did indeed seek Jesus sorrowing. Their cries might be heard a great way off

. . . They continued in prayer for over an hour, confessing
their most secret faults; and at length the agonies of some
were so strong that five of them seemed affected as those
who are in fits. (Whitefield, *Journals*, 10 May 1740)

This was no rare occurrence. A year later he described how
an entire meeting was touched:

But when we came to public prayer, the Holy Spirit
seemed to come into the congregation like a mighty
rushing wind, carrying all before it. I had not long
begun before several young men and maidens, old men
and children, were all dissolved in tears, and mourning
after Jesus. I believe there were scarcely half a dozen in
the whole congregation who were not deeply affected.
(Whitefield, *Journals*, 6 June 1741)

Again, from that November: "I had not spoken long
before, in every part of the congregation, someone or other
began to cry out, and almost all were melted to tears."
(Whitefield, *Journals*, 5 November 1741)

Such tearful responses not only revealed a profound yearn-
ing after Christ; others who were watching found themselves
also drawn to Christ:

I began to speak to them of the things of God. Their
concern increased till many burst into tears, and one fell
on the ground . . . The room was filled with the cries of
those around me, and many at that time sought Jesus
sorrowing . . . A Cherokee Indian trader who was present
desired to speak with me, saying, "I never saw or felt anything like it before." (Whitefield, *Journals*, 10 August 1741)

Jonathan Edwards found that the entire congregation would
sometimes be in tears as he preached, "some weeping with
sorrow and distress, others with joy and love" (J Edwards, *A
Narrative*, p. 14). Not only the new converts wept, for many
who had been Christians for some time "have had their love
and joy attended with a flood of tears, and a great appearance

of contrition and humiliation, especially for their having lived no more to God's glory since their conversion" (J Edwards, *Distinguishing Marks*, p. 127).

Crying out
George Whitefield also described outbursts of loud crying in his meetings:

> Preached at Nottingham, both morning and evening, with such demonstration of the Spirit and such a wonderful movement among the hearers as few ever saw before. It surprised me to see such a multitude gathered together at so short a notice, and in such a desert place. I believe there were about twelve thousand. I had not spoken long before I perceived numbers melting. As I proceeded, the influence increased till at last (both in the morning and the afternoon) thousands cried out, so that they almost drowned my voice. Never did I see a more glorious sight. Oh what tears were shed and poured out after the Lord Jesus. (Whitefield, *Journals*, 17 November 1740)

He encountered not only cries of anguish, but also cries of joy as some received direct and inner assurance of salvation:

> I then began to pray and gave an exhortation. In about six minutes, one cried out, "He is come! He is come!" and could scarcely sustain the manifestation of Jesus to his soul. The eager crying of others, for a similar favour, obliged me to stop; and I prayed over them as I saw their agonies and distress increase. (Whitefield, *Journals*, 5 November 1741)

John Wesley was equally familiar with shrieks of agony and cries of joy within a single meeting:

> After delivering the message, I called upon God to confirm His word. Immediately, to my surprise, someone nearby cried out with the utmost vehemence, as though in agony of death. We continued in prayer till a new song was put

into her mouth and thanksgiving unto our God. Soon after, two other persons were seized with strong pain and constrained to cry for the restlessness of their hearts. But it was not long before they likewise burst forth into praise to God as their Saviour. The last who called upon God, as out of the belly of hell, was a stranger in Bristol. In a short time he was also overwhelmed with joy and love.

In his own ministry in New England, Jonathan Edwards saw many outcries: "It was a very frequent thing to see a house full of outcries, faintings, convulsions and such like, both with distress, and also with admiration and joy." (J Edwards, *The Revival in Northampton*, p. 151). He also discovered that outbursts of joy were not only interrupting sermons, but also sleep:

> There have been instances before now, of persons crying out in transports of divine joy in New England. We have an instance in Captain Clap's memoirs . . . not of a silly . . . child, but a man of solid understanding, that, in a high transport of spiritual joy, was made to cry out aloud on his bed. His words are "God's Holy Spirit did witness (I do believe) together with my spirit, that I was a child of God; and did fill my heart and soul with such full assurance that Christ was mine, that it did so transport me, as to make me cry out upon my bed, with a loud voice, *He is come, He is come*."

Falling down

John Wesley frequently witnessed people fainting as he preached or prayed, falling to the ground under powerful impressions of the presence of the Spirit of God. He was earnestly inviting a response of faith after preaching at Wapping, when "many of those who had heard began to call upon God with strong cries and tears. Some sank down, having no strength remaining in them."

Wesley also records Whitefield's initial reservations about such faintings, and how he was suddenly obliged to accept their validity:

On Saturday George Whitefield and I discussed outward
signs which had so often accompanied the inward work of
God. I found his objections were chiefly grounded on the
gross misrepresentations he heard concerning these facts.
The next day he had an opportunity of informing himself
better, for no sooner had he begun to invite sinners to
believe in Christ than four persons collapsed close to him.
One of them lay without either sense or motion. A second
trembled exceedingly. The third had strong convulsions
over his entire body but made no noise other than groans.
The fourth convulsed equally and called upon God with
strong cries and tears.

Wesley's comment on this change of mind indicates his
determination not to quench the Spirit faced with the strange-
ness of these intense and even disturbing manifestations:
"From this time, I trust we shall all allow God to carry on his
own work in the way that pleases him." (J Wesley, *Journal*,
7 July 1739)

Whitefield also became accustomed to people falling down:
"Some fainted; and when they had got a little strength they
would hear and faint again. Others cried out in a manner
as if they were in the sharpest agonies of death. Oh what
thoughts and words did God put into my heart!" (Whitefield,
Journals, 14 November 1740). On one occasion as Whitefield
began to pray he saw a man drop to the ground "as though
shot with a gun" (Whitefield, *Journals*, 3 August 1741). The
next day they met privately: "I asked him what caused him
to fall down yesterday. He answered, 'The power of God's
word'" (Whitefield, *Journals*, 4 August 1741).

Jonathan Edwards used a variety of expressions to describe
this experience. One woman "almost fainted" with love when
three new converts came into her shop. When they began to
talk about Christ it was more than she could bear, and they
had to desist for her to remain upright (J Edwards, *A Narrative*, p. 58). When a group of young people, aged sixteen
to twenty-six, met at his house, so strong was the sense of
humility, self-condemnation, self-abhorrence, love and joy
that "many fainted under these affections" (J Edwards, *The*

Revival in Northampton, p. 151). One felt the need to "lie low before God" (J Edwards, *A Narrative*, p. 59). For many, when their soul was "engaged, ravished, and swallowed up", there was a resultant physical weakness – "deprived of their strength, and the whole frame ready to dissolve" (J Edwards, *Distinguishing Marks*, p. 97). He observed "many of late who have had their bodily strength taken away with a sense of the glorious excellency of the Redeemer, and the wonders of his dying love" (J Edwards, *Distinguishing Marks*, p. 127).

Not only did many people fall to the ground, some even stayed there overnight: "It was pretty often so, that there were some that were so affected, and their bodies so overcome, that they could not go home, but were obliged to stay all night where they were" (J Edwards, *The Revival in Northampton*, p. 151). Some did not merely rest in God, but received visions of heaven over many hours: "there were some instances of persons lying in a sort of trance, remaining perhaps for a whole twenty four hours motionless, and with their senses locked up; but in the mean time under strong imaginations, as though they went to heaven and had there a vision of glorious and delightful objects" (J Edwards, *The Revival in Northampton*, pp. 153–4).

Fervent prayer
A new intensity marks prayer and praise in revival. John Wesley describes prayer meetings filled with an earnest intensity:

> We met at Fetter Lane to humble ourselves before God. He had justly withdrawn his Spirit from us for our manifold unfaithfulness. Again we found God with us, as at the first. Some fell prostrate upon the ground under his power. Others burst out, as with a single mind, into loud praise and thanksgiving.

George Whitefield encountered similar fervency:

> The bitter cries and groans were enough to pierce the

hardest heart. Some of the people were as pale as death; others were wringing their hands; others lying on the ground; others sinking into the arms of friends; and most lifting up their eyes to heaven and crying to God for mercy. I could think of nothing, when I looked upon them, so much as the Great Day . . . One would imagine none could have withstood the power, or avoided crying out, "Surely God is in this place." (Whitefield, *Journals*, 15 November 1740)

A year later, the fervent response is not diminished: "Most of the people spent the remainder of the night in prayer and praises. It was a night much to be remembered" (Whitefield, *Journals*, 15 November 1741).

As if drunk

Howel Harris felt himself to be drunk in the Spirit on more than one occasion. In 1735: "Sealed by the Spirit of adoption and feeling that I loved God with all my heart, that I was in God and he in me . . . In private society till two in the morning like a drunken man. Could say nothing but glory, glory for a long time." In 1747: "God came down as he used in Wales and our hearts did burn within us." In 1749: "The Lord came, overpowering me with love like a mighty torrent that I could not withstand or reason against or doubt."

John Wesley records a further instance where the Welshman was clearly drunk in the Spirit:

Howel Harris called on me an hour or two later. He said he had been much dissuaded from either hearing me or seeing me by many who said all manner of evil of me. "But as soon as I heard you preach," he stated, "I quickly found of what spirit you were. Before you were done, I was so overpowered with joy and love that I had much trouble walking home."

Shaking

Jonathan Edwards reported that since a visit from George

Whitefield he frequently observed "great agitations of body, and an unavoidable leaping for joy" (J Edwards, *The Works*, vol 1, p. 376). At one meeting John Wesley saw twenty-six people who "trembled and quaked exceedingly". Fearing a negative reaction Wesley immediately prayed that God would prevent others from taking offence. It seemed this prayer had not been effective, for one woman "was greatly offended, being sure those so affected could stop the shaking if they wished". She was beyond persuasion, and prepared to leave in disgust. However, Wesley reported, "She had gone only three or four yards when she also dropped down in as violent an agony as the rest." While they received personal prayer, most of them were "filled with peace and joy".

Demons

As in the New Testament, when the Spirit is poured out mightily it comes as no surprise that demons begin to manifest themselves with vigorous animosity. John Wesley described a demonised woman who was hardly restrained by two or three others. Her pale face was disfigured with "anguish, horror and despair". While she shrieked as if in agony, her "stony eyes could not weep". For several hours she continued to scream out that she was lost and prayed to the devil. When Wesley and the others prayed, she would sink down as if asleep, but as soon as they paused "she broke out again with inexpressible vehemence". Shortly before 9 p.m., when Charles Wesley arrived, a second woman began to roar out with the same volume and anguish. Not till after 11 p.m. was the victory won: "God in a moment spoke peace into the soul – to the first one tormented, and then to the other. They both joined in singing praise to him who had stilled the enemy and the avenger."

On another occasion a demonised woman broke into "horrid laughter" and then the demon sought to mock Wesley: "No power, no power, no faith, no faith. She is mine, her soul is mine. I have her and will not let her go." The woman's movements became extremely violent, but they continued in prayer and she was eventually released from satanic bondage.

Children and young people

The Great Awakening impacted every generation and every class, but young people were touched more than any others. In town after town in New England the ministers made the same observation: "There have been very observable strivings of the ever blessed spirit on the hearts of many, especially the young people" (Oliver Peabody, Natick, 4 July 1743). "Many were brought under strong convictions . . . especially young people" (Henry Messenger, Wrentham, 12 August 1743). "After this, that grand and important question was in the mouths of most of my people, especially young people, What must we do to be saved?" (John Porter, Bridgewater, 12 October 1743, all quoted in Tracy, *The Great Awakening*, pp. 121–30).

Jonathan Edwards's predecessor in Northampton had seen five short periods of revival, and on each occasion "the greater part of the young people in the town seemed to be mainly concerned for their eternal salvation". Similarly, in the revivals that Edwards saw, the age group most touched were the young (J Edwards, *Distinguishing Marks*, p. 129). In particular one notorious young woman's conversion caused many to begin attending meetings (J Edwards, *A Narrative*, p. 12). While Edwards accepted that this generation seemed generally the most responsive, he also stressed that both the elderly and children had been converted, from some in their sixties and seventies to many aged nine to fourteen and one as young as four (J Edwards, *A Narrative*, p. 20).

George Whitefield reported the conversion of a young child with evident delight: "A little boy, about eight years of age, wept as though his heart would break . . . As I was going away, I asked the little boy what he was crying for. He answered, his sins. I then asked what he wanted. He answered, 'Christ'" (Whitefield, *Journals*, 5 November 1741).

Anointed preaching

The outpouring of the Holy Spirit brought a restoration of biblical preaching, with passion and with power. David Hall observed in April 1740: "And from this time I had more knowledge than ever before, what it means to preach with the Spirit and with the understanding also." Jonathan Edwards retained an emphasis on the virtues of thoughtful preparation, "strength of reason, and a good method in the doctrinal handling of the truths of religion is in many ways needful and profitable, and not to be neglected". However, he now stressed a new duty: "to raise the affections of my hearers as high as possibly I can, provided that they are affected with nothing but truth, and with affections that are not disagreeable to the nature of the subject". Perhaps wryly acknowledging his own philosophical disposition, as well as the faults of others, he observed: "an increase in speculative knowledge in divinity is not what is so much needed by our people as something else". He answered criticism of the new preaching robustly: "Some talk of it as an unreasonable thing to fright persons to heaven; but I think it is a reasonable thing to endeavour to fright persons away from hell" (J Edwards, *Distinguishing Marks*, p. 108).

George Whitefield never tired of practising and commending this new form of revival preaching. Writing to Howel Harris he advised:

Press them to believe on him immediately! Intersperse prayers with your exhortations, and thereby call down fire from Heaven, even the fire of the Holy Ghost . . . Speak every time, my dear brother, as if it was your last. Weep out, if possible, every argument, as it were, compel them to cry, "Behold how he loveth us!" (Quoted in Dallimore, *George Whitefield*, p. 75)

Personal revival

Striking examples of the intimacy with God that comes

with personal revival are provided by Jonathan and Sarah Edwards. Jonathan, whose prose style is often rather ponderously precise, reveals a great measure of emotional warmth in his personal walk with God:

. . . having alighted from my horse in a retired place, as my manner commonly has been, to walk for divine contemplation and prayer, I had a view, that for me was extraordinary, of the glory of the Son of God, as Mediator between God and man, and his wonderful, great, full, pure and sweet grace and love, and meek and gentle condescension. . . . The person of Christ appeared ineffably excellent, with an excellency great enough to swallow up all thought and conception – which continued, as near as I can judge, about an hour; which kept me the greater part of the time, in a flood of tears, and weeping aloud. I felt an ardency of soul to be, what I know not otherwise to express, emptied and annihilated; to lie in the dust, and to be full of Christ alone; to love him with a holy and pure love; to trust in him; to live upon him; to serve and follow him; and to be perfectly sanctified and made pure, with a divine and heavenly purity. I have, several other times, had views very much of the same nature, and which have had the same effects.

He also gave special emphasis to his awareness of the Holy Spirit:

I have, many times, had a sense of the glory of the Third Person in the Trinity, in his office of Sanctifier; in his holy operations, communicating divine light and life to the soul. God in the communications of his Holy Spirit, has appeared as an infinite fountain of divine glory and sweetness; being full and sufficient to fill and satisfy the soul; pouring forth itself in sweet communications; like the sun in its glory, sweetly and pleasantly diffusing light and life.

As to Sarah Edwards, for seventeen consecutive days in

1742 she had the most amazingly intense experiences of personal revival. Although she had known previous periods of personal surrender, receiving much joy and love from the Lord, these days were so striking that Jonathan asked her to draw up an account that was later included as a chapter within his memoirs (J Edwards, *The Works*, vol 1, pp. lxii–lxviii). Recognising that some might be inclined to dismiss her experiences out of hand, Sereno Dwight, the editor of the published memoirs, felt obliged to stress that Sarah was a woman of mature faith, stable in mind and enjoying full physical health. We will quote from her testimony at length because this journal, hidden within the early account of her husband's ministry, is an easily overlooked spiritual classic, describing in graphic detail what it means to know the manifest presence of God during a period of revival.

On Tuesday, 19 January, she prayed in the evening while feeling low in grace. Seeking God's help for growth in holiness, she experienced "great quietness of spirit" and "unusual submission to God", asking God to bring her spiritual aid in "his own time, and his own way". Quite simply, she yielded afresh to God, with no strings attached.

The next morning she examined herself in prayer until about ten o'clock, seeking to be dependent only on the Lord and receiving a renewed experience of peace in God. During family prayers that morning, she had a powerful impression of God's fatherly love: "I had not the least doubt, that he then sweetly smiled upon me, with the look of forgiveness and love, having laid aside all his displeasure towards me, for Jesus' sake." The immediate result was that she felt "very weak and somewhat faint". Having a strong desire to be alone with God, Sarah went to her own room. Once there she read the last verses of Romans 8, which had come to her mind in the family prayer time. Now they were "impressed on my heart with vastly greater power and sweetness still". The confidence that nothing could separate her personally from the love of God was impressed upon her with new force:

Melted and overcome by the sweetness of this assurance,

I fell into a great flow of tears, and could not forbear weeping aloud. It appeared to me certain that God was my Father and Christ my Lord and Saviour, that he was mine and I his. Under a delightful sense of the immediate presence and love of God, these words seemed to come over and over in my mind, "My God, my all; my God, my all." The presence of God was so near, and so real, that I seemed scarcely conscious of anything else.

She felt completely safe under the Father's protection, which gave her peace and happiness that was "altogether inexpressible". She experienced a deep sense of her own unworthiness, together with compassion and love for all mankind. She also felt lifted above the cares of this world. "My God was my all, my only portion."

Day and night this acute awareness of God continued until the following Saturday, when she felt that God was examining her for growth in holiness as a result of these intense experiences. That night "my soul seemed to be filled with an inexpressibly sweet and pure love to God, and to the children of God". The next few days sustained this close walk with God, together with earnest prayer for revival to break out in the town. On the Wednesday afternoon a sermon from Mr Buell, a visiting preacher, was followed by clear evidences of a fresh outpouring of the Spirit of God, in the responsiveness of the people. Sarah was "filled with such intense admiration of the wonderful condescension and grace of God, in returning again to Northampton". The immediate consequence was that admiration "overwhelmed my soul, and immediately took away my bodily strength". For the next three hours she stayed in the meeting house, sometimes in prayer for the lost, sometimes speaking earnestly with others of her great joy, often experiencing her "bodily strength overcome".

When she came home, she was eager for those present to join her in giving glory to God, "with an active, flowing and fervent heart". However, "the intenseness of my feelings again took away my bodily strength". When she recovered she began to praise God and her mind

> was so deeply impressed with the love of Christ, and a sense of his immediate presence, that I could with difficulty refrain from rising from my seat, and leaping for joy. I continued to enjoy this intense, and lively, and refreshing sense of divine things, accompanied with strong emotions, for nearly an hour; after which I experienced a delightful calm and peace and rest in God, until I retired for the night.

The next morning joy continued to well up within her. She was acutely aware of the presence of God and earnestly longed for the outpouring of the Spirit to continue and increase. By 9 a.m. she was so caught up in God that "my bodily strength was much weakened, and it was with difficulty that I could pursue my ordinary advocations". About 11 a.m. she accidentally went into the room where Mr Buell was speaking about the importance of living faith. The impact upon her was dramatic: "My strength was immediately taken away, and I sunk down on the spot." She stayed in the meeting and was then so drawn towards Christ that she "leaped unconsciously from my chair", and then "my strength failed me, and I sunk down". They carried her to her bed, "where I lay for a considerable time, faint with joy, while contemplating the glories of the heavenly world . . . I was entirely swallowed up in God, as my only portion, and his honour and glory was the object of my supreme desire and delight." This was accompanied by a "ravishing sense of the unspeakable joys of the upper world". She lay on her bed from noon till 4 p.m., "too much exhausted by emotions of joy, to rise and sit up", speaking when she could of her spiritual encouragements to the women who sat with her.

It is impossible to do justice to Sarah's experiences that night, which she described as the sweetest she ever had in her life, without quoting her at length. Her description contains the phrase that captures the heart of her personal revival – *his nearness to me, and my dearness to him*. These telling words also capture with great exactness the experiences of many believers in the present time of refreshing:

I never before, for so long a time together, enjoyed so much of the light, and rest, and sweetness of heaven in my soul, but without the least agitation of body during the whole time. The great part of the night I lay awake, sometimes asleep, and sometimes between sleeping and waking. But all night I continued in a constant, clear, and lively sense of the heavenly sweetness of Christ's excellent and transcendent love, of his nearness to me, and of my dearness to him; with an inexpressibly sweet calmness of soul in an entire rest in him . . . there seemed to be a constant flowing and reflowing of heavenly and divine love, from Christ's heart to mine; and I appeared to myself to float or swim, in these bright, sweet beams of the love of Christ, like the motes swimming in the beams of the sun, or the streams of his light which come in at the window. My soul remained in a kind of heavenly elysium. So far as I am capable of making a comparison, I think that what I felt each minute, during the continuance of the whole time, was worth more than all the outward comfort and pleasure which I had enjoyed in my whole life put together. It was a pure delight, which fed and satisfied the soul . . . It seemed to be all that my feeble frame could sustain, of that fullness of joy which is felt by those who behold the face of Christ, and share his love in the heavenly world.

The next morning, "God and Christ were so present to me, and so near me, that I seemed removed from myself. The spiritual beauty of the Father and the Saviour, seemed to engross my whole mind . . . The glory of God seemed to be all, and in all, and to swallow up every wish and desire of my heart." Around 10 a.m. Mr Sheldon came into the house and spoke of his early morning encounter with Christ: "The Sun of righteousness arose on my soul this morning, before day." Sarah's reply was marked with joy rather than one-upmanship: "That Sun has not set upon my soul all this night." Describing her night of blessing led once more to loss of all strength and "great agitation of body". For fifteen minutes she could still speak to those in the room about "the infinite riches of divine love", but then her strength failed entirely, and they carried her to a comfortable seat by the fire. Once there, she had a new sense of the presence of the power of Christ, which caused her to begin "leaping with joy and exultation". In the service that afternoon she scarcely restrained her joy: "My soul was filled and overwhelmed with light, and love, and joy in the Holy Ghost, and seemed just ready to go away from the body. I could scarcely refrain from expressing my joy aloud, in the midst of the service."

She was awake for most of the following night, with "a very lively consciousness of God's being near me" and "a constant delightful sense of God's great love". She concluded that she was prepared to do anything this wonderful God should ask of her. Only with difficulty could she refrain from waking everyone in the house that night, "when there was such a God to praise, and rejoice in". As to the following day:

> The road between heaven and my soul seemed open and wide, all the day long; and the consciousness I had of the reality and excellence of heavenly things was so clear, and the affections they excited so intense, that it overcame my strength, and kept my body weak and faint, the great part of the day, so that I could not stand or go without help.

The following evening, a liturgical phrase – "The Comforter is come" – came to her soul "with such conscious certainty, and such intense joy, that immediately it took away my strength, and I was falling to the floor". On Tuesday, Mr Buell began to speak at the dinner table of the glories of heaven and once again her strength was taken away and her limbs grew cold so that she was "to a considerable degree overcome for about an hour". As much as she could, she spoke to those around her of "my deep and joyful sense of the presence and divine excellence of the Comforter, and of the glories of heaven".

A day or two later, she was so thrilled at the mercy of God in using her husband that admiration overcame her "and took away my strength, so that I could no longer stand on my feet". A number of people visited her that Wednesday night, concerned to know how she felt. She explained that "I did not feel at all times alike, but this I thought I could say, that I had given up all to God; and there is nothing like it, nothing like giving up all to him." Others began to give testimony and then to praise God, and the results for Sarah were by now predictable: "My former impressions of heavenly and divine things were renewed with so much power, and life, and joy, that my strength all failed me, and I remained for some time faint and exhausted."

After the others left, the Spirit quickened her anew, so that she felt unable to sit still, "but walked the room for some time, in a kind of transport" with a "joyful sense of the goodness and all-sufficiency of God, of the pleasure of loving him, and of being alive and active in his service". Once again she "slept but little that night". The next morning, during a meeting given over to revival testimonies, others spoke of the "enlivening and joyful influences of the Holy Spirit on their own hearts". As she listened, "the joy and transport of the preceding night were again renewed". She "felt such intense love to Christ, and so much delight in praising him, that I could hardly forbear leaping from my chair and singing aloud for joy and exultation". She continued to be filled with joy inexpressible until the meeting finally broke up around lunch time. At this point Sarah's testimony breaks off. Perhaps she simply ran out of time to write about her intimate and awesome experiences of personal revival.

Jonathan was clearly much taken with the testimony of his wife's encounters with the manifest presence of God:

Now if such things are enthusiasm, or the offspring of a distempered brain; let my brain be possessed evermore of that happy distemper! If this be distraction; I pray God that the world of mankind may be all seized with this benign, meek, beneficent, beatific, glorious distraction! What notion have they of true religion, who reject what has here been described! What shall we find to correspond with these expressions of Scripture. *The peace of God that*

passeth all understanding: Rejoicing with joy unspeakable,
and full of glory: God's shining into our hearts, to give the
light of the knowledge of the glory of God, in the face of
Jesus Christ: with open face, beholding as in a glass the
glory of God, and being changed into the same image, from
glory to glory, even as by the Spirit of the Lord: Being called
out of darkness into marvellous light: and have the day-star
arise in our hearts? What, let me ask, if these things
that have been mentioned do not correspond with these
expressions; what else can we find that does correspond
with them? (J Edwards, *The Works*, vol 1, p. lxix)

Opposition

No work of God is without resistance and persecution, and
the Great Awakening rapidly gathered to itself not only
the hostility of some outside the churches, but also virulent opposition from churchmen who hated this evangelical
fervour with its enthusiasm for conversions and its exotic and
unseemly manifestations. Of course key leaders in the revival
were not always discreet. George Whitefield was often under
suspicion for un-Anglican behaviour, refusing to conform to
the parish system, preaching for churches in other denominations and even denouncing Archbishop Tillotson, whose
popular books soothed the mildly religious and were inimical
to the evangelical call to conversion. Though Tillotson had
been dead fifty years, Whitefield still risked the ire of the
Anglican authorities when he declared that "The Archbishop
knew no more of true Christianity than Mahomet."

Commissary Garden, a senior Anglican in the New
World, went on the attack against Whitefield, lambasting
his "slander and defamation" against Tillotson. Whitefield
had denounced the cruelty of the slave owners, and Garden
also rallied to their defence. He charged that the orphanage
that Whitefield had set up when he first came to Georgia was
a place of cruelty and exploitation. He also linked Whitefield
with every fanatic he could think of, including a notorious
cultic family who practised incest and even murder. Above

all, Garden held an ecclesiastical court, the first ever held outside England, in which he attempted to suspend Whitefield
from public ministry. Whitefield appealed to the High Court
in London, which never bothered to hear the case, and his
personal response to Garden was typically robust: "I pitied,
I prayed for him, and wished the Lord would convert him"
(quoted in Dallimore, *George Whitefield*, p. 93).

Jonathan Edwards's chief opponent was Charles Chauncy,
who later became a Unitarian. Chauncy spoke of the
Awakening as mere "commotion". He considered the claim
that everyone needs to be born again to be censorious and
arrogant, championing the conventional view that everyone
should be considered a true Christian unless damnable
heresy or scandalous immorality could be found in them.
By demonstrating that heretical and cultic groups had
experienced manifestations such as those described above,
Chauncy sought to discredit the revival, implying that such
phenomena could only arise from "enthusiasm or impos-
ture". While not denying that some good had been done,
he dismissed the revival as predominantly ill-conceived,
destructive, even evil. Though Edwards does not mention
Chauncy, this controversy provided the context for his own
enduring reflections on revival. Years later Edwards had to
face more painful, personal opposition, when the church
members in Northampton, who had been served by him
through several periods of revival, decided to remove him
from office. He had sought to introduce church discipline,
excluding from communion those whose lives showed no
evidence of personal salvation and continuing commitment
to Christ.

Edwards freely acknowledged that some scoffed and ridi-
culed the revival, comparing "what we called conversion, to
certain distempers" (J Edwards, *A Narrative*, p. 15). He was
at pains not only to argue against such opponents, not least
Chauncy, but also to address those who remained hesitant,
not wishing to take sides or form a hasty judgment.

A long continued silence in such a case is undoubtedly
provoking to God; especially in ministers. It is a secret

kind of opposition, that really tends to hinder the work. Such silent ministers stand in the way of the work of God, as Christ said of old, "He that is not with us is against us." (J Edwards, *Distinguishing Marks*, p. 132).

Back in Britain, William Seward became known as "the first Methodist martyr" when he died after a mob inflicted severe injuries on him at an open-air meeting in Wales. Welsh mobs may have been particularly vicious. Howel Harris was also struck on the head while in Wales, "with violence enough to slit my head in two". Although in time he mended physically, his mental faculties never fully recovered.

For John Wesley, persecution grew into a way of life. John became used to Anglican clergy refusing access to their pulpits, on the ground that he was beside himself. Riots, peltings with dirt and stones, farm animals set loose in the crowds, all were part of the standard bill of fare for an itinerant evangelist. Libellous verses were sung beneath the brothers' window:

> Charles Wesley is come to town,
> To try if he can pull the churches down.

Mobs gathered, perhaps most notably at Walsall and then Falmouth, demanding Wesley gave himself into their hands. On both occasions, as the crowd drove him through the town, his death at their hands seemed inevitable. Reading his journals, the only reasonable explanation for his long life is frequent, miraculous preservation by the living God.

Call to prayer

Isaac Watts and John Guyse wrote the preface to the first British edition of Jonathan Edwards's *A Narrative of Surprising Conversions*. They confidently declared that they had never come across such a mighty work of God "since the first ages of Christianity" (J Edwards, *A Narrative*, p. 1). They also acknowledged the sad contrast with recent experience in both Britain and North America. For many years there had been a general complaint that "the work of conversion goes on very slowly" (J Edwards, *A Narrative*, p. 2).

Above all their words are an urgent call to prayer and repentance, which must surely find an echo in our generation:

> Certainly it becomes us, who profess the religion of Christ, to take notice of such astonishing exercises of his power and mercy, and give him the glory which is his due, when he begins to accomplish any of his promises concerning the latter days: and it gives us further encouragement to pray, and wait, and hope for the like display of his power in the midst of us . . . but we have reason to fear that our iniquities, our coldness in religion, and the general carnality of our spirits, have raised a wall of separation between God and us . . . "Return, O Lord, and visit thy churches, and revive thine own work in the midst of us." (J Edwards, *A Narrative*, pp. 2–3)

Chapter 4

TIMES OF REFRESHING
– A FRESH TOUCH IN TORONTO

As a child I once persuaded my father to film me swimming in a river. With careful editing the home movie was fairly impressive, but in fact I was still an incompetent beginner, as yet unable to sustain more than three or four strokes. All too often as Christians we kid ourselves with similar self-deceptions, playing at church in the safety of the shallows, content to paddle despite Jesus's invitation to launch out into the deep. For some, a visit to Toronto had been a first step. For us, it was a consummation of what God had already begun. It was as if Claire and I had learned to swim in a shallow pool, and now we were being invited to take a leap into deep water.

Already we had received so much during the 1994 wave of the Spirit. Every few days in London there were fresh testimonies and news of more churches being touched. With every day we saw, heard and marvelled at the increasing intensity of what God was doing. At this stage, others began encouraging us to make the trip to Toronto. David Rosser, a senior leader with Scripture Union, had seen his vicar and his wife, David and Mary Pytches, make the trip. They had just returned from Canada and the impact upon their church had been immediate and immense. His advice was categorical: "There's nothing for it, Rob: you should drop everything and go."

I have always been wary of jumping on the latest Christian bandwagon, and some who know me well were surprised at my eagerness to make the trip. However, by now I needed no convincing that God really was at work in increased power and it was already widely recognised that the Airport Vineyard had become a fountainhead of blessing in the English-speaking world. What churches in Britain were only beginning to savour, the Airport Vineyard had been immersed in since late January. We wanted to encounter this visitation of the Spirit at its most intense, where there had been opportunity for the outpouring to increase and the response to mature.

Visiting the place of an outpouring to learn and receive is nothing new. Jonathan Edwards wrote of men visiting Northampton, Massachusetts on business who ended up taking revival home with them. As the news spread, church leaders deliberately made the journey, to see, learn and receive (J Edwards, *A Narrative*, pp. 15–18). Like wildfire in a sun-scorched forest, the revival spread from church to church. As we see God at work in greater measure, our faith is enlarged and our lives empowered. Revival is a spiritual contagion: if you visit those who have got it, you may well catch it too.

Hurdles to cross

The hunt for air tickets proved arduous. Travel agents were at a loss to understand the sudden demand for short stays in Toronto. Just as things looked hopeless a friend offered help with more expensive tickets and the trip was suddenly on. We drove to the airport full of expectancy, knowing that we were travelling to Toronto at God's invitation. We knew we had much to learn and, far more importantly, we believed that the Holy Spirit had much for us to receive.

The first three days in Canada each brought an unwelcome surprise. During the flight I lost an unexpected battle with a grittier than average granary roll. One moment I removed a stone-hard grain from my mouth. The next it was followed by a large shard of tooth. A third of one of my molars no longer had a home. With urgency I prayed that our short visit would not be sidetracked by severe toothache or an emergency visit to a dentist. Fortunately what remained of my tooth held up for the rest of the trip.

The next day brought a car crisis: the car we had planned to hire proved suddenly unavailable. The international company's adverts suggest that nothing is more simple than hiring a car, but we had arrived in Toronto during a Canadian national holiday and phone calls to all the major rental companies left us still bereft. All we could do was to pray hard and take a cab to the airport, in the hope that someone might cut short their trip and return a car early. The line of rental desks all told the same story. "Sorry, no cars available" declared the sign at the first and second booths. The third was even more stark: "No cars in Toronto." Another urgent prayer as we walked towards Avis, the last desk in the line.

"Do you have any cars available?"

"Yes, just the one. Would this be suitable?"

At that moment I was ready to hire anything from an East European rust bucket to an army surplus tank. A gleaming white Oldsmobile with just a couple of hundred miles on the clock would be very suitable indeed. We drove back to our motel filled with relief and gratefulness. God's last-minute provision had tested our faith but exceeded our expectations.

The next morning brought the third shot across our bows. Claire woke up with a sore eye, took one look in the mirror and burst into tears. We had never seen anything like it. She looked as if she had just come from the make-up room for the latest Sylvester Stallone boxing movie. The area around her eye was swollen like half a peach, the eye itself shut fast, lost within the swelling. Only sunglasses hid her embarrassment when we set off for the Sunday morning service at the Airport Vineyard. That meeting was the mountain top of our visit, when we would move from being sympathetic observers to full participants.

First impressions

The first evening had been about fighting jet lag, as we

tried to convince our weary bodies that it wasn't really an unearthly hour in the morning, British Summer Time. Struggling to keep my eyes open I gazed around the Airport Vineyard's premises, a warehouse with seating for about 400, near the end of the international airport runway. For those used to massive gothic edifices, such a church building comes as quite a culture shock. Nonetheless, such premises have a number of advantages when it comes to making modern people feel at home. The style of design is *familiar and contemporary*, looking just like many people's work place, when many traditional church buildings are so ancient and remote. The furnishings are *comfortable*: the main meeting room is fully carpeted, with comfortable seating and air conditioning, in contrast to the draughts, pews and bare floorboards that still face the visitor in many traditional church buildings. The premises are *functional*, designed to serve the immediate purposes of the church, not shackling today's believers within the constraints of a previous generation's priorities. What's more the building is *provisional*. A servant of the church, it can easily be disposed of when the time comes to move to a larger site.

Unimpressive at first sight, the building had definite advantages. I appreciated its simplicity, which resonates well with the culture and values of the baby boomer generation. The inconspicuous ordinariness of the premises reminded me of an observation made by Martyn Lloyd-Jones some thirty-five years previously, that since revival is a work of God, the Holy Spirit very often begins a revival not in a church that is large and well-known but in one unknown, of modest size and premises.

The atmosphere was immediately striking. Even before the meeting began, an overwhelming sense of expectancy filled the air. The buzz in a crowd awaiting the Queen or a film star at a movie premiere paled into insignificance beside it. This heightened sense of anticipation was certainly not for the worship band or the preacher: it was for the outpouring of the Holy Spirit. Never before had I been in a room with such an intense awareness of God's presence in power. There was no hype, no working people up, just a simple recognition that we had met together for "times of refreshing from the presence of the Lord".

The high tide of living waters stayed at full flood for every meeting. If the level of expectation was mountainous, there was an Everest of manifestations. The reason for this was plain: the manifest presence of God was utterly arresting, immediate and awesome. Some trembled lightly or were shaking vigorously even before the meeting began. Others cried out, with anguish or with joy, particularly during times of prayer and the preaching. At the end of the meeting, the invitation for personal prayer was immediately followed by the removal of all the chairs. This proved absolutely necessary, because at each meeting the entire floor became littered with bodies. I was reminded of Martyn Lloyd-Jones' description:

> Suddenly they are aware of his presence, they are aware of the majesty and the awe of God. The Holy Spirit literally seems to be presiding over the meeting and taking charge of it, and manifesting his power and guiding them, and leading them, and directing them. That is the essence of revival. (Lloyd-Jones, *Revival*, p. 100)

The range of reactions was enormous: right next to each other were people rejoicing in Christ, weeping over their sin and receiving peacefully. Any in need of a drink or a quick bite to eat slipped out to a small coffee bar, freely disengaging from the meeting. In short, while the experiences of meeting with God were overwhelmingly strong, there was no sense of emotional pressure, let alone frenzy, no obligation to stay to the very end of the meeting, nor to respond in exactly the same way as everyone else. I had never seen so many people receiving so richly. This was awesome. This was God.

Around the edge of the room stood others who were at liberty to observe in cautious detachment for as long as they needed. Jonathan Edwards noticed a similar pattern during the revivals in Northampton:

> Having heard various and contradictory accounts of it,

they were careful when here to satisfy themselves; and to that end particularly conversed with many of our people; which they declared to be entirely to their satisfaction; . . . Mr Lord told me that, when he got home, he informed his congregation of what he had seen, and that they were greatly affected with it; and that it proved the beginning of the same work amongst them, which prevailed till there was a general awakening. (J Edwards, *A Narrative*, p. 8)

At the leaders' meeting the following Wednesday, John Arnott, the senior pastor, told the story of how the time of refreshing had begun. In May 1992 and July 1993 Mark Dupont had received prophecies in which the Lord promised a mighty outpouring of the Spirit upon Toronto. With others in the Airport Vineyard, John was experiencing an increasing sense of spiritual thirst: the church was healthy and growing, but transfer growth was proving easier to come by than adult conversions. Over these months John sought personal prayer from a number of leaders, including Benny Hinn. In November 1993 he attended a conference organised by men prominent in the Argentinian revival. There, he received prayer from one of them, Claudio Freidzon, an Assemblies of God pastor and former professor of theology. Claudio's church had grown to 2,000 within four years. But still he sought more from the Lord. After Claudio had a powerful encounter with the Holy Spirit during personal prayer ministry, the church rapidly doubled in size while his wider evangelistic ministry increased. Claudio is convinced that the heart of revival is found in seeking God's presence: "The anointing comes through the praise and worship. God's presence descends as we immerse ourselves in adoring him."

During the same year of 1993 another Vineyard pastor, Randy Clark, had been feeling drained and near to spiritual burnout. However, when he met John Arnott he described his personal revitalisation through the ministry of South African evangelist, Rodney Howard-Browne. John was so impressed by Randy's testimony that he asked him to lead a series of meetings at the Airport Vineyard beginning on

20 January 1994. The rest is history. God broke out upon the church in great power and the time of refreshing has continued and intensified ever since. When we made our visit there were meetings every night except Monday, with additional prayer meetings, a Sunday morning service and a leaders' meeting on Wednesday afternoons. The Airport Vineyard has seen over 30,000 Christian visitors including several thousand pastors. Far more importantly they have seen a steady and increasing flow of conversions, with new professions of faith every week.

Throughout our stay the testimonies confirmed the impression that the Holy Spirit was flowing with unusual liberty and power. Some testimonies from previous weeks were retold to us in the coffee bar. One minister had been watching warily at the edge of the room when suddenly he felt overcome by the presence of God and, drunk in the Spirit, he slipped slowly and irresistibly to the floor. Another, on his return home, was typing up the order of service for the following Sunday. As he typed the first line of a hymn, "Come Holy Spirit", the Spirit of God came upon him afresh and he sank to the floor once again.

Some of the most memorable testimonies were those given during the evening meetings. Two elderly couples spoke of driving up from Texas thirsting to receive. One of the women had begun to laugh before the Lord, then the others joined her. Their physical frailty was apparent as they gave testimony, but in their spiritual being they had been strengthened and refreshed. Their faces shone with holy joy. After giving testimony they received prayer and one by one they rested in the Spirit, three on the floor and one man in his wheelchair. A couple of days later one of the men gave further testimony of physical healing from a urinary disorder.

A whole family gave testimony, children of about nine and eleven speaking of wonderful encounters with the love and power of God. They showed neither fear nor embarrassment as they spoke about shaking and falling to the ground. One night a young man who had planned a heavy drinking session in a nearby bar decided at the last moment to stick his head inside the door of this church, where strange and curious things were said to happen. Although he may have come to stare and be amused at the follies of religious fanaticism, he was completely overwhelmed by an undeniable awareness of God's presence and reality. The next day he came back, and surrendered his life to Christ. Others spoke of coming to Toronto feeling dispirited by the trials and disappointments of church life. Some were losing vision, others were worn out. Still others came burning with zeal and eager for more. In case after case, though the emotions and manifestations varied enormously, the core of the testimony remained constant: "I have met with the Lord, and he has restored my soul!"

Strengths and weaknesses

What then did I make of this remarkable church? God is undeniably at work in great power and I wanted not only to see and receive but also to assess and learn. Several of their leaders said that the Holy Spirit had "ruined them for the ordinary". Putting up with the usual poor substitutes for the Apostolic church, the mediocre and the mundane which typify normal church life, had become completely unattractive. They could no longer compromise with such pale and insipid imitations, in the light of their dynamic experience of the real thing.

The sheer volume of outsiders has exacted a high price. As a fountainhead of blessing in the western world, the Airport Vineyard has received an unprecedented number of visitors. In the days of travel on horseback and a population of a mere 250,000 in New England, Jonathan Edwards could know personally those who came to observe the outpouring of the Spirit in Northampton. In the modern global village, the volume of visitors to Toronto quickly exceeded anything more than a rough head count.

The preachers, worship leaders and prayer ministry team have given an enormous number of hours every week in order to serve many they neither know nor will ever meet again. During their Sunday morning service it was freely acknowledged that many have experienced the pain of recognising that they have lost something of their own church in the task of serving the wider Church. Nonetheless, one of the most striking and admirable qualities of this church is their servant heart. Worn out some may be and certainly they have sacrificed their own convenience and comfort, but they are bubbling with eagerness to give away everything the Holy Spirit has given them. With the same extravagant generosity with which God has blessed them, they are eager to be instruments of God's blessing to as many others as possible.

As servants of the wider Church, they show a complete lack of possessiveness of this work of God. Never in their meetings did anyone from their church describe what is happening as the "Toronto blessing". Such a slogan is an unhelpful one, despite its current vogue in Britain, distracting from the fact that this is not an event organised by men and women, but a mighty work of God. What's more, in every meeting they strenuously emphasised that they had no desire to lay claim to this outpouring for the Vineyard churches alone: the closer to God we grow, the more indifferent we become to denominational labels.

Naturally there were weaknesses to learn from, not least because they were even more overstretched in summer, when the exodus of their own people on holiday was paralleled by an increased number of visitors, particularly whole families from Canada and the States. The Airport Vineyard emphasises the personal touch in prayer ministry, with team members prepared to spend considerable time helping an individual to "soak in prayer". Sometimes, however, the sheer crush of people meant this ideal could not be followed, and prayer became more of a production line. The majority of those providing ministry showed both spiritual authority and sensitivity in the way they prayed: one or two, however, were flapping their arms like windmills, misguided zeal overtaking wisdom as they sought to give the Spirit a heavy helping hand. Similarly, while the vast majority who received were concentrating only upon Christ, there were some who, I suspected, were probably manifesting in the flesh. This should hardly be surprising: I have come across no other church which is entirely free from the tares of misguided zeal and fleshly responses.

Another difficulty was apparent among a few of the visitors, who were so thrilled and excited by what God was doing that their enthusiasm was prone to break out in ways completely unrelated to the worship or preaching in that particular meeting. This too is nothing new, for Jonathan Edwards discovered that when the Spirit is poured out freely, church leaders require more discernment than ever before: "But when the people were raised to this height, Satan took the advantage, and his interposition, in many instances, soon became very apparent: and a great deal of caution and pains were found necessary to keep the people, many of them, from running wild" (J Edwards, *The Revival in Northampton*, p. 154).

Turning from these minor weaknesses, I was thrilled by God's superb strategy in using a church in Toronto, a city once described by Peter Ustinov as "New York run by the Swiss". Even popular tourist guides have to acknowledge that this is, to say the least, a quiet capital, with a reputation not so much for excitement or grandeur as for being rather sensible and staid. If New York is a wild teenager, Toronto often seems more like a maiden aunt. So why should a Vineyard church in Toronto be strategic? Canadians pride themselves on being different to Americans. They consider themselves to be quieter, more reflective. This makes their culture a kind of halfway house between the States and Europe, and gives it an intermediate character and style with which both Americans and Europeans can feel at ease. If the refreshing had started in the States, the manifestations would probably have been more noisy and even harder for some Europeans to handle. If the refreshing had started in England, we would have been greatly tempted by imperialistic pride, as if the best things always start here! What's more, the United Nations has identified Toronto as the most ethnically diverse city in the world. Nowhere could be better for a worldwide spiritual movement to begin.

As to denomination, the Vineyard movement has become a stream where everyone meets, from Pentecostal to Anglican, from historic Free Church to New Church. In short, to begin this outpouring in the English-speaking world at a Vineyard church in Canada, with easy access by air, is more shrewd and effective than any human strategist could have devised. Canada and the Vineyards have become cultural and denominational intermediaries for just about everyone: until the refreshing takes strong root elsewhere, all roads will lead to the Airport Vineyard, Toronto.

Receiving power

I said earlier that the decisive turning point for Claire and me came on Sunday morning. We enjoyed the service a great deal, appreciating the warmth of both the welcome and the worship. In the ministry time Claire was the first of us to receive, and fell peacefully to the floor. I continued to wait for prayer, knowing that God had something more for me, but not knowing quite what. "May I pray for you?" came the customary request. As a hand was laid upon my head a jolt of power surged through my body. Once as a teenager I had given myself a mild electric shock, but the force of this surge was countless times greater. As the Spirit of God continued to charge me up, I heard a heavenly voice declare: "This is your anointing with power."

I nearly cried out in awe and wonder, then fell to the floor and continued to shake and tremble as God's manifest presence electrified my life. It seemed that the scales were falling from my eyes and the Spirit was restoring my first zeal for Christ, my first hunger and vision to serve him with all that I am. A rekindled passion burst into flame for God and his glory. I yielded my life to Christ with fresh eagerness: "Lord, I'm ready to go for broke. I want to receive all that you want to give, and do anything you want, go anywhere you want. There's no limit!"

When I finally got up from the carpet, Claire was already sitting in a chair waiting for me to come round. The ministry time seemed nearly over and we hugged each other in delight at all that God was doing in our lives. Then I glanced back at her badly swollen eye: in the heat of the moment she had forgotten to ask for healing prayer. A member of the prayer team was nearby, so Claire went over and explained her need. He was about to pray when he suddenly paused and said, "You're a pastor's wife, aren't you?" She nodded. "Well, there are some other things the Lord is inviting me to pray about first."

As he began to pray for Claire she quickly fell to the floor. He knelt beside her and continued to pray, as the Holy Spirit began to pinpoint some acute and deep-rooted cares and pressures. Unrealistic and excessive demands and negative, critical attitudes had been dumped on Claire over the years, and they had begun to grow like thorn-bushes around her heart. A gentle person bruises deeply. As the Lord drew off the hurt and pain, he poured into her life anew the Spirit of hope and love with the result that, after extensive prayer, Claire lay resting peacefully on the floor, many wearying and crushing burdens lifted from her life, her soul refreshed and restored. Only after this unexpected ministry was complete was Claire's sore eye eventually prayed for. As we drove back to the hotel Claire was very tired but had a new lightness of spirit. As for her eye, by mid-afternoon the disfiguring swelling had completely disappeared.

These amazing encounters could not yet be termed a full-blooded revival. They are still a time of refreshing in the presence of the Lord. But what a refreshing! No words describe our experiences better than Martyn Lloyd-Jones's summary of what happens when God comes down in power:

It is a consciousness of the presence of God the Holy Spirit literally in the midst of the people . . . It is all above and beyond the highest experiences in the normal life and working of the Church. Suddenly those present in the meeting become aware that someone has come amongst them, they are aware of a glory, they are aware of a presence. They can not define it, they can not describe it, they can not put it into words, they just know that they have never known anything like this before. Sometimes they describe it as "days of heaven on earth" . . . God has come down amongst them and has filled the place and the people with a sense of his glorious presence. (Lloyd-Jones, *Revival*, p. 306)

That evening we received further ministry, inking over this new liberation and empowering by the Spirit of God. The next day was the Airport Vineyard's day off, so we visited Niagara. We saw the falls from every angle we could, but most memorable of all was standing behind the magnificent Horseshoe Falls in a disused power station tunnel, gazing in wonder at the water's massive force and volume. At an ordinary waterfall such a position would face you with a curtain of water. But at Niagara thirty-four and a half million gallons of water roar and race down the torrent every minute. This was no curtain; it was a fortress in motion.

Previously we would have been content to praise God for the beauty and dynamism of this marvel of creation, a deafening, exhilarating, awesome encounter with a power beyond human control. But now we saw Niagara with new eyes, for here was the ultimate metaphor for the outpouring of the Spirit of God in revival power. Even so, Lord, will you send your Spirit for world revival. Not little by little or drop by drop, but a living torrent to revive your Church, that the world might awake and believe!

More, still more

Our return to London brought one further hindrance. For the first time ever our baggage was lost. By now Satan's hand was overplayed and there was no way we would let such a hitch deflect or distract us from all that God had begun. That Sunday Claire gave testimony in our church, and then I prayed for her. She began to laugh lightly, caught up in holy joy, then fell peacefully to the floor. During the ministry times that day we prayed for more people than ever before, and it was not until late evening I was able to receive prayer myself. Once again I began to tremble and fell to the floor, where the shaking became more intense. The revelation of God's power was wonderful and yet fearful. It felt as if an electrode had been attached to each of my fingertips and to my ears, which grew numb as the sensation of power continued to increase. So intense and acute was this sensation that I began to wonder whether I was about to die. Later that night I concluded that this was the Spirit's specific anointing to write this book, which I began in earnest the next day.

The next afternoon the Spirit of God came upon me again and I began to shake. I left my word processor and found Claire in the kitchen. "Claire, I think I am meant to pray for you." While Claire was resting on the carpet I was given a prophetic word for her: "The days of your sackcloth and mourning are ended." The next day Claire went to the leaders' meeting at Wimbledon. When she came home she was eager to interrupt my writing to describe a vivid picture she had seen while resting on the floor. There stood before her a solid wooden panelled door with wrought iron fittings. The key was in the lock, but the door was shut and locked. She asked the Lord to show her what it meant, and then the door opened. At first all she could see was darkness. Gradually the darkness lifted and there came into sight an exquisite garden, full of beautiful flowers in full bloom with a wonderful, manicured lawn. The beauty of the garden stretched as far as her eyes could see. Claire still felt she didn't understand, and so she asked the Lord to show her more. Then she realised that the garden had been there all the time, hidden in the shadows cast by the closed door. What's more, the key had always been in the lock. She had been cooped up in the house, constrained and hemmed in. But now that she had opened herself to all that the Lord was doing, she was set free to enjoy the heavenly garden of blessing and delight.

When Claire finished describing her vision, a Scripture immediately came to mind that sums up God's invitation, both to Claire and to all believers:

> The creation waits in eager expectation for the sons of God to be revealed . . . the glorious freedom of the children of God.
>
> (Rom 8:19, 21)

As God pours out his Spirit in refreshing, he wants to fulfil our spiritual potential and liberate us from our man-made prisons. He longs to set us free and open every door that is locked against the free flow of the love and power of the Holy Spirit. God's wonderful purpose at present is to prepare us not only for our ultimate home in heaven, but also for days of heaven on earth. The Lord is preparing his Church for revival.

Chapter 5

TEARS, JOY AND LAUGHTER

What are we to make of all the emotional and physical reactions to the present work of God? For some, every strong response is a further confirmation of the Spirit's power. For others, every tear, every laugh, and the thud of every falling body confirms that this could not possibly be anything to do with God.

Within the Bible there is no apology for frequent expressions of strong emotion. Feelings are an integral part of living faith. From a biblical perspective, relationship with God involves the whole person. As a result, we are not only called to love God with our minds, but also with our hearts. It is hardly surprising that the Bible speaks of emotional responses to the living God. When we first fall in love, most of us experience intense emotion. We speak of "walking on air" and our hearts can feel literally enlarged with romantic ardour. I have a friend who literally jumps for joy whenever his football team scores a goal. Faced with danger we experience feelings of fear and may well shake or shiver with emotion. Even so, if our emotions and bodily reactions can be intense when faced with earthly love, joy or fear, how much more can we expect emotional and even physical responses to a powerful encounter with the presence of the living God.

Fear

We turn first to fear because, in a familiar Old Testament

refrain, the fear of the Lord is the beginning of wisdom (Ps 111:10; Prov 1:7, 9:10). The fear of the Lord is also a frequent and central command of the law, coming four times in Leviticus (19:14, 25:17, 25:36, 25:43) and seven times in Deuteronomy (6:2, 13, 24; 10:12, 20; 31:12, 13). Such fear does not come from a merely conceptual belief in the existence of God, but from a full-blooded recognition of the reality of God, both in his holiness and as the judge of all. The Apostle Paul quotes from Psalm 36:1 in his diagnosis of what is wrong with human society: "There is no fear of God" (Rom 3:18). The fear of the Lord is pure (Ps 19:9) and those who fear him lack nothing (Ps 34:9). To fear the Lord is to hate evil (Prov 8:13), and those who know God have no need to fear evil (Ps 23:4), nor disaster (Ps 49:5, 112:7; Prov 3:25), nor the reproach of men (Isa 51:7). Ultimately, all people will come to fear the Lord (Ps 64:9, 67:7).

Just as the books of law and wisdom commend the fear of the Lord, personal encounters with the living God can provoke powerful sensations of fear. When Moses meets with God at the burning bush he is afraid (Exod 3:6). When Isaiah sees a vision of God at the temple in Jerusalem he cries out in fear: "Woe to me! I am ruined! For I am a man of unclean lips, and I live among a people of unclean lips, and my eyes have seen the King, the LORD Almighty" (Isa 6:5). Similarly Daniel makes no apology for revealing that a powerful supernatural encounter caused him to be terrified, with the result that he fell to the ground (Dan 8:17).

These fervent, intense and immediate responses to God are paralleled in reactions to Jesus's ministry. The disciples cry out in fear when they see him walking on water (Matt 14:26). When he calms the storm, they are filled with fear and amazement (Luke 8:25). After the man possessed by a legion of demons has been delivered, the people gather and ask Jesus to leave their area, because they are overcome with fear (Luke 8:37). While Jesus's authority to bring about miracles and deliverance generates an immediately fearful reaction, he urges people not to fear those who can kill the body but only God, who "after the killing of the body, has the power to throw you into hell" (Luke 12:5). Even as Jesus's demonstrations of God's power evoke fear, he points to the need to fear the awesome power and authority of God, the ultimate Judge.

Luke's Gospel begins with Zechariah, startled and gripped with fear when he encounters an angel of the Lord (Luke 1:11–12). It is hardly surprising that the angel's first words need to be "Do not be afraid." This seems to be almost the standard greeting of angelic visitors, not as a polite gesture but out of necessity. Contrary to popular opinion derived from school nativity plays, the usual first reaction to angels is not to cherish them as decorative or pretty, but rather to be terrified! Later, when Luke wrote the book of Acts, he continued to record expressions of fear in response to supernatural manifestations. After Ananias and Sapphira come under divine judgment, great fear seizes the church and all who hear about it (Acts 5:5, 11). After Saul's conversion, the church throughout Judea, Galilee and Samaria enjoys a time free from persecution, and as the Holy Spirit strengthens and encourages the believers, they grow in numbers, living in the fear of the Lord (Acts 9:31). When Cornelius distinctly sees an angel, he stares at him in fear (Acts 10:3, 4). When Paul is in Ephesus, he is able to provide healing and deliverance in the name of Jesus. However, when the sons of Sceva try to copy his techniques without his personal faith in Christ, they experience humiliating consequences, left bleeding and naked by the violence of a demonised man (Acts 19:11–18). As a result those living in Ephesus are "all seized with fear", not simply at the power of evil but at the greater power of the name of Jesus. As Luke records, "the name of the Lord Jesus was held in high honour" (Acts 19:17). The church that knows the holiness of God will also know something of the fear of the Lord. The church that experiences demonstrations of God's power will also discover some measure of fear before God's mighty acts.

Tears

Turning from fear to tears, the Bible is one place where it's certainly not the case that big boys never cry. In the Old Testament there are references to weeping all night (Ps 6:6), the tears of the oppressed (Eccles 4:1), tears of disgrace (Isa 25:8) and tears of longing in exile, by the rivers of Babylon (Ps 137:1). As to individuals who weep, we find a biblical who's who. Esau wept in his rivalry with Jacob (Gen 27:38). Jacob wept with Esau in a wary reconciliation (Gen 33:4), and later wept at the presumed death of his son Joseph (Gen 37:35). When Joseph was preparing to reveal his true identity to his brothers, he wept so loudly that it became a talking point among the Egyptians (Gen 45:2). Soon he wept with his brothers (Gen 45:14–15), and when Jacob finally arrived in Egypt, Joseph threw his arms around his father and "wept for a long time" (Gen 46:29). Later, he wept over Jacob's corpse and wept again over his father's last request to forgive his brothers fully (Gen 50:1, 17). Ruth and Naomi wept together (Ruth 1:9) and Hannah wept as she longed for a child (1 Sam 1:7). Saul the first king of Israel wept (1 Sam 24:16), as did David and Jonathan (1 Sam 20:41). On one occasion David's army wept aloud all day long until they had no strength left within them (1 Sam 30:4).

In the New Testament, there are also plenty of tears. Jesus wept at Lazarus' tomb (John 11:35), he wept over Jerusalem (Luke 19:41) and he prayed with loud cries and tears concerning his crucifixion (Heb 5:7). A prostitute wiped Jesus's feet with her tears (Luke 7:38). Peter wept bitterly after his threefold denial of Christ (Matt 26:75). Paul also knew the place and value of tears. He described his ministry as serving the Lord with great humility and tears (Acts 20:19) and he continually warned with tears against false teachers (Acts 20:31). He wrote a stiff letter to the Corinthian church, with great distress, anguish of heart and many tears (2 Cor 2:4). With tears he wrote to the Philippians of those who live as enemies of the cross (Phil 3:18). The Ephesian elders wept as they embraced Paul before his final departure from their region (Acts 20:37). When Paul wrote to Timothy he remembered with fondness Timothy's tears at their last meeting (2 Tim 1:4).

It's not just that biblical people are able to express

themselves freely through weeping. There is also a great deal of praying with tears. Hezekiah prays for mercy with tears (2 Kgs 20:2–3). The tears are clearly taken seriously by God since Isaiah is given the message that the Lord has not only heard his prayer but has also seen his tears (Isa 38:5). The Psalmist weeps at the lawlessness of Israel (Ps 119:136) and also speaks of weeping and fasting (Ps 69:10). Job weeps before God (Job 16:20). Malachi speaks of people in great distress literally weeping on the altar (Mal 2:13). Above all, Jeremiah is the prophet of tears. He frequently weeps for Israel, even as he brings dire warnings of impending judgment, and cries out for mercy in tears (Jer 9:1, 18; 14:17; Lam 1:16, 3:48). On occasion it is difficult to discern whether the prophet speaks in his own voice or in the voice of the Lord, and so in Jeremiah's prophecies it is also possible to speak of the weeping of the Lord over his rebellious people.

Tears are also a sign of the revival of faith in Israel. Jeremiah foretells a time when the people will seek the Lord with tears (Jer 50:4). Similarly Joel calls the people to renew a right walk with God:

> "Even now," declares the LORD,
> "return to me with all your heart,
> with fasting and weeping and mourning."
>
> (Joel 2:12)

Wherever in the Bible we find depth of feeling, in close relationships, in intercession, in repentance and in serving God, there tears and weeping are likely to be expressed.

Longing and delight

The Psalms speak of a deep longing for the things of God: a longing for God's law and commands (Ps 119:20, 131) and a longing for God's salvation (Ps 119:81). As a deer pants for streams of water, the awakened soul thirsts after God, for he is the only one who can satisfy (Ps 42:1). Even the wild animals are said to pant for God (Joel 1:20).

This longing for God is linked in the New Testament to our future hope. The letter to the Hebrews speaks of a "longing for a better country – a heavenly one" (Heb 11:16). Paul describes Christians groaning inwardly as they await eagerly their entry to heaven (Rom 8:23). The only adequate way to describe such intense longing is to speak of a passion and hunger for God. Such passionate faith cannot possibly be detached, philosophical or theoretical. It simply demands to be warm-blooded and heartfelt.

"Delight" is another biblical word that expresses a strong emotional dimension to both life and intimate relationship with God. Those opposed to God find delight in doing wrong (Prov 2:14), in mockery (Prov 1:22) and in war (Ps 68:30). They also delight in abominations (Isa 66:3), in wickedness (Hos 7:3) and in lies (Ps 62:4). The Lord on the other hand delights in kindness, justice and righteousness on the earth (Jer 9:24). He delights in obedience more than in burnt offerings (1 Sam 15:22). God's commitment to economic fairness is expressed in his delight in accurate weights (Prov 11:1). There is also a divine delight in showing mercy (Mic 7:18). The men of Judah are the garden of his delight (Isa 5:7), and he delights in the well-being of his servant (Ps 35:27). In Isaiah's prophecies of the suffering servant, God identifies the servant as the one above all in whom he delights and upon whom he will pour out his Spirit (Isa 42:1). However, while the delight of God is specifically applied to Christ (Matt 12:18), God also promises to take delight in all who serve him:

> The LORD your God is with you,
> he is mighty to save.
> He will take great delight in you,
> he will quiet you with his love,
> he will rejoice over you with singing.
> (Zeph 3:17)

As to our delight in the things of God, in the Old Testament there is delight in the Temple (Ezek 24:21), in Jerusalem (Isa 65:18) and in the Sabbath (Isa 58:13). The Jews delight in

God's mighty acts in history (Ps 111:2), particularly their deliverance (Ps 78), vindication (Ps 35:27) and salvation (Ps 35:9). There is delight in the fear of the Lord (Isa 11:3) and abundant delight in the revelation of the law of the Lord (Pss 1:2; 112:1; 119:16, 24, 35, 47, 70, 77, 92, 143, 174). Above all, there is not only delight in revering the name of the Lord (Neh 1:11), but also delight in the Lord himself:

> Delight yourself in the LORD
> and he will give you the desires of your heart.
> (Ps 37:4)

The Apostle Paul adds two further dimensions of delight. Looking at himself, he delights in his own weakness, for this sharpens the focus of his dependence on grace in all things (2 Cor 12:10). Looking at other believers, he delights in their evidence of firm faith and growth in Christ (Col 2:5).

The frequent use of this word "delight" demonstrates that living faith in the Bible cannot be understood as merely belief in God or formal religious observance. Rather we are presented with lives centred upon an absorbing and pleasurable walk with God. Where God's person, works and revelation are the focus of our attention, the soul will delight in the richest of fare (Isa 55:2).

Joy

The Bible has so much to say about joy that we can only turn to a few highlights. We must begin by stressing that the joy of the Lord is *abundant*. In all, the Bible contains 218 references to joy, of which fifty-three are found in the Psalms. To speak of joy alone seems often to be inadequate, and so we find thirteen references to great joy, three to celebrations of joy and three to everlasting joy. As if to redouble its measure, joy is also frequently paired with gladness (fourteen references). So central to God's good purposes for creation is the response of joy that the trees, fields, rivers, mountains, heavens and angels are all said to express joy before the living God.

Joy is also *exuberant*. Jewish joy is not a quiet, inward disposition, nor is it the power of positive thinking, but it is expansive and often noisy. This strong emotional response to God finds ready expression in making music and in songs of joy (twenty-seven instances). The whole body is involved through leaps of joy (Luke 6:23) and dances of joy (Jer 31:13). Great banquets before the living God are described as feasts of joy (eight references). This is not to be confused with the starched and stilted formal rigidities of an old-fashioned English wedding reception. When the Jews had a feast of joy they really knew how to enjoy themselves!

Outbursts of biblical joy are not only found in music, but frequently in shouting. Although familiar in a football crowd, such volumes of noise have often been taboo in church. When we began to invite local primary schools to visit our buildings one of the first things the teachers told the children to do was to speak quietly. It's as if their God is an old man with particularly sensitive ears. We grow up with the idea that only hushed tones are acceptable, and even ordinary levels of speech are inappropriate or even irreverent. Ezra and Nehemiah both report that, at the time of the restoration of Jerusalem, shouts of joy blended with an outcry of weeping. So great was the noise that it could be heard far away (Ezra 3:12–13; Neh 12:43). The book of Job reveals that even the angels shout for joy (Job 38:7). Why should joy before the Lord be expressed so vigorously? Because it is natural to do so and what is more, it does us good. As we declare it with our voices, our joy increases within us.

The Old Testament doesn't merely permit shouting should it prove absolutely necessary and unavoidable on very exceptional and rare occasions. Shouting is positively commended and commanded. The Old Testament contains no less than twenty-seven references and invitations to "shout with joy before the Lord". Though it may seem astonishing, there are as many biblical references to shouting with joy as to singing with joy. Some say that modern worship is too noisy, but the real question is this: where has all the shouting gone? Maybe we have little understanding of biblical shouting because we have yet to receive a biblical measure of joy.

It hardly needs saying that such abundant and exuberant joy is deeply felt. When I first started going to church I couldn't get used to the chant in which the congregation declared, "And let your chosen people be joyful." It was sung in neutral, flat tones, almost as a lament or dirge. One thing was sure, we hadn't received much joy so far, and we certainly didn't expect any rapid or significant improvement in our emotional condition! In the Old Testament the joy of the Lord is described as our strength (Neh 8:10), inspiring us and keeping us going. God brings joy to the heart (Ps 4:7, 19:8) and to the soul (Ps 94:19). The heart leaps with joy in God's presence (Ps 28:7) and even throbs and swells with joy as God moves in power (Isa 60:5). There is an anointing with the oil of joy (Ps 45:7), and God has the power to exchange mourning and sorrow, tears and sackcloth for a new season of heartfelt joy (Esther 9:22; Pss 30:11, 126:5; Isa 35:10, 51:11; Jer 31:12, 13).

As to Jesus, he is full of joy through the Holy Spirit (Luke 10:21). He promises to give his joy to believers (John 15:11), a joy that cannot be taken away (John 16:22). Jesus prays for all believers to receive joy in full measure (John 17:13) and explains that answered prayer will result in abundant joy (John 16:24). Not only is joy a fruit of the Spirit (Gal 5:22), but the Spirit also wants to fill us with joy (Acts 2:28, 13:52; Rom 15:13; 1 Thess 1:6). Some believers experience an overflow of joy, which leads to great generosity (2 Cor 8:2). Love between Christians increases our experience of joy (Phil 2:2; Philem 1:7; 1 John 1:4; 2 John 1:12). This joy can become so intense and overwhelming as to be inexpressible and full of glory (1 Pet 1:8). At the end of time, this joy will see its final consummation, when we are presented before the Father with great joy (Jude 1:24).

We have become so frosted over in our emotions that we suffer a paralysis of the heart. If we come across even a glimmer of biblical joy it is likely to seem well over the top. This is not because biblical joy is excessive, but because most Western churches have suffered for generations from an excessive absence of joy. Our perspective is woefully distorted. We are like a man who has lived in Alaska for

so long that he complains that English summers are too hot.
We have lived with so little joy for so long that we are likely
to find it hard to recognise and receive the real thing. But
still the Spirit of the Lord comes bearing gifts of abundant,
exuberant and heartfelt joy, not merely on the surface of our
lives but in the depths of our being.

Twin excesses

When we are considering the rightful place of emotions in
living faith, the twin positions of excess are emotionalism
and those forms of Christianity that are as dry as dust. Emotionalism, which is emotion-centred and emotion-driven, is
a grave distortion of the gospel, however well intended.
All that matters is the emotional froth, and as people
work themselves up or are manipulated by their leaders,
froth is usually all that anyone receives. Those trapped in
emotionalism are chasers after experience, always hungry
for new sensations. The direct results are preaching without
substance and Christians without stability. An emotionalist
is like a drug addict: living for the next emotional high, with
no time for the pursuit of real personal growth. Christianity
with no head is a denial of two major human resources, the
gift of reason and God's revealed truth.

Emotionalism leads inevitably to fanaticism. Where emotions are the centre of attention, some will begin to base
new doctrines upon their emotional experiences. The biblical
pattern reverses this order. We are not filled with joy and
then create new teachings based upon a vacuous experience.
Rather, as the Spirit of God is poured out upon us, old truths
are bathed in new joy. We do not seek emotions, we seek
to meet with God. But where God is met in his glory and
his grace, his power and his love, there cannot possibly be
an adequate response that does not include an expression of
real emotion. As Finney observed, "Great revivals of religion
can never exist without deep excitement of feeling" (Finney,
Reflections on Revival, p. 121). It is absolutely crucial that
we recognise the vital distinction between right response to

God and excess, between a heart kindled by the outpouring of the Spirit which brings home the love of Christ and mere emotionalism which is an end in itself.

As to emotionalism's implacable opposite, dry as dust Christianity claims that it is centred on Christ and his cross, rather than any emotional response. In practice, however, this formal religion is a barren land, excluding not only emotionalistic excess but any emotion at all. Every expression of an emotional response is considered inherently suspect and indisputably ill-advised. In such a culture, it is hardly surprising that David Watson used to observe, "Emotionalism is not the chief peril of the English clergy." For many of us, the more immediate risk than emotionalism is that we baptise the stiff upper lip which has been so much a part of English society and schooling. As a result vital Christianity is mutated into something rigid, cold and completely undemonstrative. We urgently need to grasp the truth that the correct response to an excess of emotion is not an absence of emotion but a right and biblical emotional response to God.

Martyn Lloyd-Jones spoke frequently and with urgency about the place of feelings in biblical Christianity, above all in revival. He was dedicated to preaching the Word of God, but he never allowed the ardent use of the mind in studying Scripture to become an excuse for a lack of godly passion:

> You cannot read the accounts of the revivals of the past without observing that the emotional element was always prominent. But, today, so many are terrified of emotion and have almost a phobia concerning excesses. Indeed I fear that it can be said of many that they seem to be so afraid of what they call excesses that they are "quenching the Spirit". When have you known a congregation to be really moved? When have you heard a congregation crying out? . . . Are you explaining away the great phenomena accompanying the revivals of the past in terms of the 20th century, and saying that the people at Llangeitho listening to Daniel Rowland were a sort of primitive people, lacking education, and just emotionalists? The

Apostle Paul reminds the elders of the church at Ephesus of how he preached "with tears". And Whitefield used to preach with tears. When have you and I last preached with tears? What do we know, to use the phrase of Whitefield, about preaching a "felt Christ"? Is not this the cause of the trouble today? (Lloyd-Jones, *The Puritans*, p. 189)

The Apostle Paul warned about such paralysis when he foretold that in the last days some would hold strenuously to the form of religion, while denying its power (2 Tim 3:5). The direct results are preaching without passion and Christians without zeal. Christianity that is all head and no heart is a shallow travesty, a dead orthodoxy, no matter how polished and sound its theological abstractions. Just as the only body with no emotions is a dead body, the only faith with no emotions is dried up, withered, and on the brink of extinction.

Weeping

The key emotional responses when God moves in power are expressions of great sadness and great joy. Perhaps the most common response of all is tears. For some, tears are an expression of an acute sense of unworthiness when we are humbled before the mightiness of God. More often, tears are an expression of intense repentance, a deep sorrowing before God for the weight of our sin. Not that sorrow is the only cause of tears. Some people weep whenever they receive a gift. Others weep whenever they hear the words "I love you". In the same way, whenever there is a great outpouring of the Spirit of God, a profound touch of love will lead to weeping. For some, the weeping expresses sheer delight in the extravagant love of God, full of mercy and grace. For others, their life has been starved of love, often through difficult relationships with their parents or in adult life. As a result, receiving the love of God is such a wonderful contrast that the overflow of joy is almost painful and can only be expressed through tears.

In the present time of refreshing I have seen tears for all these reasons. Good leaders are not remotely interested in making people cry just for the sake of an emotional response, but when God moves powerfully, for many people the natural response will include spontaneous weeping. I think of one woman who always cries when she senses the presence of God. For her the tears are not a sign of some profound encounter, but simply of preparation – an openness to God. For Jim, his regular tears seem to be a special gift of the Spirit. He weeps in response to the wonder and love of God, and he weeps just as much in intercession for the needs of others.

I also think of two men whom I have only seen weep once. Though the reasons were quite different, for both the context was a powerful personal encounter with God. In a meeting where almost everyone else was caught up in abundant and overflowing joy before the grace of God, I saw Ron lying face down, his head on his arms. When he eventually got up, he testified how God had been humbling him, revealing afresh his pride and self-sufficiency and causing him to renew his dependence upon the living God. David came forward after a sermon on the Spirit of adoption to ask for prayer for a fresh revelation of God's Father heart. After waiting on God for some minutes, tears suddenly started from David's eyes and his voice cracked with depth of feeling, as he cried out with an intimacy he had never entered before, "Abba, *my* Father!" When he began to meet for the first time at depth with the immediacy of God's fatherly love, his heart melted and the tears began to flow.

Laughter

Before the present outpouring of the Spirit I was familiar with a tearful response to God. The difference in recent months has been that we have seen more tears shed, and in particular a greater number of men weeping. But I had never previously seen laughter before God. I was familiar with seeing people, as Charles Wesley's hymn puts it, lost in wonder, love and praise. I was used to seeing some with radiant and seraphic smiles, whether during worship or after receiving personal prayer. But the laughter came as quite a surprise.

Taking delight in God with laughter is certainly commended in the Old Testament. When Abraham had the promise of a son confirmed, he fell face down and laughed as he began to take the promise in (Gen 17:17). At the birth of her promised son, Sarah gave him the name Isaac, which means laughter, and declared: "God has brought me laughter, and everyone who hears about this will laugh with me" (Gen 21:6). One of Job's friends' more useful attempts to help is the promise that God will bring restoration: "He will yet fill your mouth with laughter and your lips with shouts of joy" (Job 8:21). When the Jews were liberated from Babylonian captivity and were finally able to return to Jerusalem, the Psalmist describes, with fond enthusiasm, an abundant overflow of holy joy:

When the Lord brought back the captives to Zion,
we were like men who dreamed.
Our mouths were filled with laughter,
our tongues with songs of joy.

(Ps 126:1–2)

At first laughter sprang up almost silently. Some who had rested in the Spirit, whether in a chair or on the floor began to laugh aloud, clearly but quietly, as if someone had turned the sound down. Then, at a London leaders' prayer meeting, I saw a number of believers almost splitting their sides with loud guffaws, laughing with great volume and vigour, absolutely captivated by joy in the Lord. Back in our own church I soon saw for the first time a complete prayer meeting convulsed in laughter. It began with one or two, but it was so infectious that in the end almost everyone was laughing fit to burst. Of the two who weren't laughing, one was resting peacefully before God, the other was weeping. I was laughing so much that tears ran down my face, and as I looked around the room, others were equally filled with joy. For me, the most precious gift of laughter was given to my wife, and I will repeat the details briefly. Claire is soft-spoken and in everyday life her laughter is quiet too. She might have been embarrassed if the Lord had asked her to laugh noisily, but when the Lord suddenly touched her with laughter, her joy was deeply felt but quietly expressed. Laughter and tears welled up from the depth of her being, till she fell to the floor peacefully, captivated by the wonder of God's personal and infinite love.

Laughter does us good. When someone is downcast or worn out, hearty laughter can bring a sense of release. Some have even suggested that laughter is healing, ironing out the worries and stresses of modern living. So why laugh before God? What we have begun to experience is not some cheap, earthly, indulgent or irreverent laughter. This is holy joy. An overwhelming sense of the goodness of God and the wonder of salvation. Our souls have been delighting in God and feasting on his presence. In a world which is captive to anti-supernaturalist assumptions, treating God as a redundant concept, the presence of the living God is breaking through once more. As Charles Wesley put it, the joy of heaven has to earth come down.

Before the present outpouring of the Spirit I would have found the idea of holy laughter very strange. Could it be nothing more than mass hysteria or self-indulgence? My recent personal experience, and that of many others, simply doesn't fit such a category. This outbreak of laughter is an emotional expression of a biblical principle: in God's presence there is fullness of joy (Ps 16:11). Once we are filled with such joy, one of its natural outlets is laughter. Such laughter knows no irreverence, no flippancy. So wonderful is the joy, so captivating the splendour of God, that laughter has become a natural means of expressing the abundancy of life and love in Christ. Just as the Apostle Peter promised, we experience times of refreshing in the presence of the Lord. As a result, sometimes with tears and sometimes with joy and even laughter, we are learning to take a deeper delight in the living God.

No one in the New Testament expresses such experiences

more clearly than Peter: "Though you have not seen him, you love him; and even though you do not see him now, you believe in him and are filled with an inexpressible and glorious joy" (1 Pet 1:8). In my early days as a Christian we were taught to rationalise away such feelings. Joy was reduced to a settled and confident state of mind, trusting in the cross of Christ. To be sure, our joy begins with God's mercy in the sacrifice of his Son. But this abundance of joy beyond words is of a different order to sound evangelical convictions or even charismatic bounciness. Here is a joy that comes from God. A joy that wells up within. A joy that characterises churches that are either in revival or are being prepared for it.

It is impossible to have an adequate response to the Gospel of Christ that excludes the emotions. There is no grasp of grace without wonder and joy. There is no receiving God's love or falling in love with Jesus without a heartfelt response. Christian faith cannot live by feelings alone, but when John Wesley and George Whitefield preached, they preached with passion and they preached to touch the emotions, not solely the mind. When Whitefield wept as he spoke of the cross his was not a mind enslaved to emotional excess but a heart captivated by the wonder of God's mercy. Truth was on fire as they spoke of hearts strangely warmed and the need to know the felt Christ within.

It sadly remains the case, in our day as in theirs, that some believers so concentrate on avoiding excess that they seem incapable of allowing the proper place to any emotional response. Through fear of emotionalism they exclude every last hint of heartfelt response to Christ. We must reject such extremism as strenuously and bluntly as possible: the church that chooses to be emotion-free chooses also to be revival-free. When the Spirit is poured out abundantly upon the Church, the presence of God will warm the heart of every believer . . . except for those who refuse to receive.

Chapter 6

FALLING AND SHAKING

Years ago, when I first heard about people falling down in prayer I was very dismissive. I simply couldn't see the point. The temptation of cynicism prompted me to suspect that they were almost certainly pushed to the floor. Failing that, I mused, either they throw themselves deliberately or it must be a form of mass hysteria. My instinctive prejudices found it easier to believe in a human or satanic cause than in the possibility that God could move in such a way. Both biblical study and personal experience have altered my opinions and overcome my instinctive hang-ups. On the one hand, I saw biblical precedent for this sort of manifestation. On the other, I began to see people fall down when I prayed for them – and I knew that I never pushed anyone! In the present move of God we have seen a considerable increase in falling down, and so some careful explanation is required.

Falling in the Bible

So who fell down in the Bible? In John's vision of heaven, the elders fall down and worship before God (Rev 4:10; 5:8). From this vision we may say that one kind of falling down is a conscious posture, presumably face down, in which the physical act of self-abasement is an expression of submission and adoration by the whole person, body and spirit.

A second kind of falling down that is involuntary and unplanned occurs in both the Old Testament and the New. When God manifested his presence upon Mount Sinai,

Moses bowed to the ground and worshipped (Exod 34:8). Similarly, Abraham fell face down before powerful revelations of God (Gen 17:3, 17). On several occasions Ezekiel encounters a dramatic vision of the glory of God. The invariable result is that he fell face down. It seems that all strength had drained from Ezekiel's body, or that he had no intention of moving without express permission, because on three separate occasions he remains lying down until either the voice of God commands him to get up or the Spirit of God assists him to his feet (Ezek 2:1, 3:24, 43:5). In the case of Daniel, as Gabriel approaches near, overcome with terror he falls prostrate. As the angel speaks, Daniel rests in a deep sleep, only returning to his feet when the revelation is complete and he is given express permission (Dan 8:17–18).

In the New Testament when Peter, James and John see the bright cloud of God's glory and hear his voice at the transfiguration, they fall face down, terrified before the divine presence (Matt 17:6). The conversion of the Apostle Paul was brought about by a direct encounter with God's glorious presence: "Suddenly a light from heaven flashed around him. He fell to the ground" (Acts 9:3–4). This is not Paul's last such experience. We don't know how often he fell down in prayer, but we do know of another major experience: "When I returned to Jerusalem and was praying at the temple, I fell into a trance, and saw the Lord speaking" (Acts 22:17–18). In the trance, Paul receives words of personal guidance from God, urging him to leave Jerusalem in haste, because his testimony will not be accepted there, and calling him to mission among the Gentiles (Acts 22:18–21). Similarly, the book of Revelation begins with a vision of the risen Christ, to which John's response seems best described as a physical collapse: "I fell at his feet as though dead" (Rev 1:17). Now if you fall as though dead there is no time for the tidy niceties of assuming a correct and neat liturgical posture. Here are men overwhelmed by the awesome presence of God. The instantaneous response to their intense spiritual encounter is to collapse to the ground.

The exact position in which Paul and John came to rest

– face down or face up, flat out or in a crumpled heap –
is not mentioned, presumably because it is irrelevant. We
can therefore conclude that whether people fall forwards
or backwards today is quite immaterial. What matters is to
meet with God in a direct and powerful way. For both men,
the most important results were concerned with salvation
and discovering God's eternal purposes. The immediate
physical result was much less important, but remains quite
unmistakable: when God revealed himself powerfully, they
came crashing to the ground.

One clue to all this falling down is found in the Hebrew
word for God's glory. *Kabod* is a word that carries the
implication of the weighty presence of God. A glorious
manifestation of the divine so immediate that you could
almost touch God. A presence so substantial, so awesome,
that it can quite overwhelm those who encounter God in
this way. The glory of God came down so powerfully when
Solomon opened the first temple in Jerusalem that the
prepared worship had to be abandoned and the priests were
unable to complete their planned rites (1 Kgs 8:10–11). The
same glory overwhelmed Moses and Ezekiel, Paul and John,
causing them to fall to the ground. Where God manifests his
glory today, we can expect the same physical reactions to be
repeated.

What happens after falling down follows a variety of
patterns. Whereas Ezekiel is made to get up before he
receives verbal instructions, Paul hears a voice while he is
on the ground, and only when the voice from heaven has
finished is he given permission to stand up (Acts 9:6). In
the same way, after Daniel has fallen he describes himself
as being in a deep sleep. However, while he is resting
physically, he has a heightened spiritual awareness as he
receives supernatural revelation. In the case of both Paul
and Daniel the falling to the ground is no more than the
beginning of their encounter with God. Once they are there,
they enter a deep state of spiritual receptiveness in which
God speaks to them directly, while to any observers they may
appear to be asleep or even in a trance. This doesn't mean
that we should attempt to induce trance-like conditions – to

empty the mind is an occult practice, opening the individual indiscriminately to spiritual forces. Our task is to concentrate on Jesus Christ and receive from him; for some, the result will be not only falling down, but also hearing from the Lord or even receiving a vision. However, we cannot rule out the possibility of a trance induced by the Holy Spirit, since Paul testifies to exactly this kind of encounter in Jerusalem, as did Peter at Joppa: "He fell into a trance" (Acts 10:10).

Falling in revivals

We saw in Chapter Three that "fainting in the Spirit" became a familiar experience in the Great Awakening. Subsequent revivals saw not only repetition but even an increased frequency of this manifestation. Thomas Rankin wrote to John Wesley about a revival in Virginia in 1776:

> . . . such power descended, that hundreds fell to the ground, and the house seemed to shake with the presence of God . . . Look wherever we would, we saw nothing but streaming eyes, and faces bathed in tears; and heard nothing but groans and strong cries after God and the Lord Jesus Christ. My voice was drowned amidst the groans and prayers of the congregation. I then sat down in the pulpit; and both Mr Shadford and I were so filled with the divine presence, that we could only say, "This is none other than the house of God! This is the gate of heaven!" (*The Arminian Magazine* (USA) 11, p. 563)

In 1788, Philip Bruce described a further outbreak of revival fires in Virginia:

> . . . vast numbers flocking into the fold of Christ from every quarter. In many places in this circuit, as soon as the preacher begins to speak, the power of God begins to be present; which is attended by trembling among the people, and falling down; some lie void of motion or

breath, others are in strong convulsions; and thus they continue, till the Lord raises them up which is attended with emotions of joy and rapture. (Quoted in Murray, *Revival and Revivalism*, pp 80–1)

In the Kentucky revival at the turn of the century, the intensity of the outpouring of the Spirit led to similar responses. Many dropped "as if shot dead", some remaining prostrate for a considerable length of time. Those who had been dismissive of such behaviour were known to come under the power of God and fall to the ground themselves, some crying out in repentance for their former hardness of heart. As many as 800 were seen to fall to the ground at a single meeting. One minister gave an eyewitness account which reveals his own struggle to come to terms with such dramatic responses:

In time of preaching, if care is taken, there is but little confusion: when that is over, and the singing, and praying and exhorting begins, the audience is thrown into what I call real disorder. The careless fall down, cry out, tremble and not infrequently are affected with convulsive twitchings. Among these the pious are very busy, singing, praying, conversing, falling down in extasies, fainting with joy. (Quoted in Murray, *Revival and Revivalism*, pp. 166)

Richard M'Nemar's account of a camp meeting in June 1801, with an attendance of some 4,000, shows how an overwhelming sense of the presence of God not only led to protracted meetings, where the ordinary priorities of life were abandoned in the face of such a dramatic outpouring of the Spirit, but also to the sudden eruption of these manifestations in everyday living:

The meeting continued five days, and four nights; and after the people generally scattered from the ground, numbers convened in different places, and continued the exercise much longer. And even where they were not collected together, these wonderful operations continued

among every class of people, and in every situation; in
their houses and fields, and in their daily employments,
falling down and crying out, under conviction, or singing
and shouting with unspeakable joy, were so common, that
the whole country round about, seemed to be leavened
with the spirit of the work. (Richard M'Nemar, *The
Kentucky Revival* or *A Short History of the Late Extraordinary Outpouring of the Spirit of God* (New York,
1846) pp. 24–5)

Charles Finney described how falling down was an initial
and dramatic sign of revival breaking out in one church where
he was preaching:

I had not spoken to them in this strain of direct application
more than a quarter of an hour when all at once an awful
solemnity seemed to settle down upon them. The congregation began to fall from their seats in every direction and
cry for mercy. If I had had a sword in each hand I could
not have cut them off their seats as fast as they fell. Indeed,
nearly the whole congregation were either on their knees
or prostrate in less than two minutes from this first shock
that fell upon them. Everyone who was able to speak at all
prayed for himself. (Finney, *Autobiography*, pp. 82–3)

Finney had to break off preaching and began to pray with
individuals who had become convicted of sin and desperate
for certain salvation in Christ. His own heart "was so
overflowing with joy at such a scene . . . It was with much
difficulty that I refrained from shouting and giving glory to
God." Although Finney had to leave them mid-evening to
fulfil another appointment, God's presence had come down
with such force that they continued to pray throughout the
night. The next morning they had to vacate the building for
the sake of the local school, and so they moved hastily to
a nearby house. There they were still unable to break up
the meeting and called Finney back to speak to them again.
This amazing meeting continued until late afternoon (Finney,
Autobiography, pp. 82–3).

Making sense of falling

What phrase best describes all this falling down? "Slain in the Spirit" is striking and graphic, and it certainly captures John's experience of falling down *as though dead*. But to many ears, including mine, it sounds unduly hostile and threatening, not to say destructive. One eyewitness of revival made a startling comparison that is certainly graphic but has, not surprisingly, never become a customary description: "stout men fell as though a cannon had been discharged and a ball had made its way through their hearts" (quoted in Murray, *Jonathan Edwards*, p. 167). In the 1859 revival in Northern Ireland they called it being "struck". As Martyn Lloyd-Jones explained, "It was exactly as if a person had been literally struck or hit upon the head, with the result that they fell to the ground in a state of complete unconsciousness" (Lloyd-Jones, *Pevival*, p. 134). We need a phrase that encompasses the variety of prostrations that we come across. My favoured term used to be "resting in the Spirit", but I have come to prefer an old revival phrase: **"falling under the power of God"**.

Although some will fall down involuntarily and swiftly return to their feet, for many people the real benefit of meeting with God seems to come not in falling down as such, but in the subsequent time of remaining on the floor in his presence. For some this is accompanied by further physical manifestations of trembling or even vigorous shaking. For others, this resting before God is very quiet and tranquil, not only externally but also in the inner being. There is a peace that passes understanding in the powerful presence of God. Seeing Paula resting on the floor Carol admired her tranquillity: "She looks so peaceful, just like a baby."

"Yes," I replied, "and that's just how you looked half an hour ago!"

Once we enter into new encounters with God, new questions and problems arise. If you have been mightily blessed by falling spontaneously to the ground, it is tempting to give others a helping hand, forcing them to fall over too. Such nudges or shoves help no one and only hinder or impede the true work of God. Norman Moss helpfully counsels against trying too hard: "You are inviting the Spirit to come. You are not conducting traffic or becoming a human windmill." As a result of the distractions of such misplaced zeal, some leaders have adopted a "no touch" policy when they pray in this way, in order to avoid any possibility of misunderstanding or misrepresentation. Even if this policy seems over-cautious, great care needs to be taken that touch is always appropriate and sensitive. The laying on of hands gives no excuse for heavy-handedness, nor for any stroking or massaging.

It's not just the people offering prayer who can be over-enthusiastic, for with similar misplaced zeal some who seek prayer may hurl themselves to the ground. They may be trying to help God, to imitate others or to draw attention to themselves, whether consciously or unconsciously. The intentions may be good or they may be self-serving. Whatever the reasons, such displays are a waste of time. With such people it helps either to ignore them until they get up of their own accord, or to have them taken to a separate room if they are becoming a distraction, or even to encourage them privately but firmly to get to their feet.

That's not to say that choosing to be prostrate before God is wrong. It's a posture that's to be welcomed as a uniquely evocative and expressive act of self-abasement before God's awesome majesty. The problems arise when someone tries to copy the external symptoms of someone else's encounter with God. External conformity is empty, futile and completely misses the point: falling over does not guarantee a blessing. What matters most is a personal meeting with God. Only God knows what external manifestations are appropriate for an individual, and only God should be in a position to determine what will come about. In the same way, we must always speak out firmly against the temptation to suggest that those who fall over have entered the premier league of spirituality. Our walk with God is all of grace. Falling over is neither a reward for good behaviour nor a proof of spiritual superiority. This line of argument will be familiar to many, because leaders in renewal have been making exactly the same points about tongues as a gift of grace for many years.

So do we have to fall over to receive a full blessing? No. Physical symptoms are never presented in the Bible as compulsory, and so we cannot claim that falling over is a necessary or vital experience for every believer. If a church embraces such a policy, what results is a spirituality that is guaranteed to be hopelessly shallow. In the past I have come across churches where it seems that everyone falls over for about ten seconds and then returns to their seats. To me this sounds more like liturgical gymnastics than truly resting in God! In the same way, standing to receive prayer cannot be made obligatory. Personal freedom of choice is important. There's not much point standing for prayer if the only reason is that it has become a compulsory posture. If you are fighting the posture, it might be better not to stand at all.

For a few people, it is inconceivable that God would lay them out on the floor from a standing position – their frail bodies couldn't take it. I know one elderly lady with arthritic knees who frequently rests in the Spirit while sitting in a chair, sometimes when no one else has been touched, sometimes when the floor around her is littered with fallen bodies. Nonetheless, while it is by no means compulsory, we are learning to encourage believers to stand when receiving prayer. In this way we leave open before God the possibility of falling or not falling. When God is moving in great power, not everyone is able to stand. Kate came forward for prayer, but so powerful was her sense of the presence of God that she only got halfway to the front before she sank into a chair and rested in God. Jim managed to get to the front, but then sank to his knees and was quite unable to stand, overcome by God's glory. Later, from his kneeling position he fell forward and lay prostrate, weeping before his Saviour.

Misunderstandings abound among Christians inexperienced in powerful outpourings of the Spirit. Some churches have adopted the policy of explaining what's going on, briefly but clearly, at every meeting. Just as some may misunderstand by throwing themselves enthusiastically to the floor, others misunderstand by locking their knees and engaging in an act of wilful defiance – "Lord, I'm asking you to pour the Spirit upon me, but I absolutely refuse to fall over!" When Steve confessed this attitude he realised it had left him concentrating so much on retaining his defiant and rigid posture that he made neither space nor time to receive from God. I'd much rather someone either gives God carte blanche to do whatever he chooses, or otherwise simply sits down, thus avoiding altogether the possibility of a dramatic fall. Refusing to fall over is as much a waste of time as throwing yourself to the ground: both excesses impede the free flow of the Spirit of God. If someone is fearful, let them receive sitting. Next time they may have grown in confidence before God and be able to receive when standing.

What about a catching team? On the one hand, if catchers are in evidence, people may think that falling over has become compulsory. As a result some may conform to expectations in an empty way, while others defy and even take offence at what they perceive as undue pressure. On the other hand, when God moves in power, many people will quite genuinely and spontaneously fall to the ground. Some have no fear of falling, and keel over whether or not anyone is near to hand to cushion their fall. Indeed, some claim never to have been hurt in the slightest when falling in this way. Others are more cautious and may even have a deep-seated fear of falling, whether from fear of injury or fear of looking of foolish. For these folk, the knowledge that someone is there to catch them if needed can ease their anxiety. It doesn't mean that they have to fall, but if they feel themselves beginning to go they won't have to fight it and jerk back upright over and over again, for as long as prayer is continued. I have seen some people stumble and stagger across a room, torn inwardly between their response to the work of the Spirit and their fear of falling. On balance, it seems to me helpful to have a team of catchers, especially in a period of outpouring of the Spirit when many are falling over. Of course, it still needs to be clear that catchers are a precaution, and no one will mind if those prayed for don't need to use them, either because they stay upright or because they fall too quickly to be caught.

The catchers don't need to do anything except let the person know they are there, most naturally by lightly brushing a hand against their back if they begin to rock. I once came across an over-zealous catcher who was rocking people vigorously. I resolved that if he started on me I would speak out quickly: "I want you to let go, stand back and give room for the Holy Spirit to work freely." In my church he would have been corrected firmly and no longer used if he didn't mend his ways.

In the past, if someone fell over we tended to turn to pray for the next person, as if the one who had fallen had more or less finished receiving their blessing. In the present wave of the Spirit we have learned to continue to pray for those on the floor, helping them to receive all that God has for them in their time of refreshing. For many people, the temptation is to get up too soon. In our spirit we can be communing with God, while in our mind we may from time to time become detached from the experience, wondering along these lines: "I feel a bit of a fool down here, I wonder if I should get up yet." It is far better to wait for divine permission to stand up than to be impatient to be back on your feet.

John came for prayer feeling very dry and distant from God. After prayer he fell to the floor and rested before God. When he began to get up he still looked rather sleepy and the prayer team felt he was rushing back to his feet. As he propped himself up on his arms we raised hands towards him and prayed quietly in tongues. Within seconds he fell back on to the carpet and remained there until he was truly ready to get up. We usually encourage the person not to get up in a hurry, but sometimes this advice is superfluous. "Stay on the floor as long as you need to," I reassured Sue as she opened her eyes. "I couldn't get up if I wanted," she replied. "It feels as if God has pinned me to the floor until he's sorted me out!" Not everyone who falls over experiences such a sensation, but for some it seems to be the spiritual equivalent of a general anaesthetic, allowing sufficient time for God to perform spiritual surgery, a deep work of renewal or healing in their inner being.

There is tremendous variety in a time of refreshing.

Anthony came for prayer and didn't fall over. In fact he showed no sign of outward response. As I prayed I had a picture of a dried up pot plant, on to which water was being poured. The water was running straight through the flower pot and into the saucer below. I described the picture to Anthony, explaining that I believed God needed to soak him over and over to restore his soul. A fortnight later he gave testimony with a radiant face. God had begun to make his presence felt, at work and at home, and Anthony had a restored hunger for God and his Word. Others fall once, and in a single moment God provides a major personal blessing. Still others fall regularly over a period of several weeks or months. For some the subsequent falling seems like a series of echoes, receding from a climactic moment. For others, each time they are overcome by the Spirit of God there is a deepening encounter, as God continues to press home abundant life upon them. Cath phoned me for advice: "Rob, every time I pray I rest in the Spirit. What should I do?" My reply was simple: "Keep praying and keep receiving. But you'd better not pray too much in office hours at the moment!"

Most who fall do so while praying, but a few fall without any conscious preparation or warning. I heard of one woman who came under the presence of God in the supermarket and fell to the floor. Picking herself up quickly, she tried to brush off the incident to a man stacking the shelves with a simple explanation: "I must have slipped." As she began to walk away, she realised this evasion was dishonouring to God. With a deep breath she went back and explained what really happened. "I didn't think you could have slipped," the shelf-stacker replied. "Those who do usually want to sue us. But what you have said is amazing, and I'd like to come to your church to see for myself!"

Not even journalists are exempt from the touch of God. The present manifestations have resulted in several eye-witness accounts in the national press. Some have naturally been cynical and dismissive. But on one occasion a journalist writing for *The Times* visited the Vineyard Church in Putney. As she drank coffee at the side of the meeting, she began to feel dizzy, her hand shook, and there was a sudden sense of the infinite in the school hall. She left in a hurry, reckoning that if she stayed any longer the presence of God would sweep her to the floor.

When Jonathan Edwards reflected on the physical manifestations he noted two contrasting emotional contexts: "either those who have been in great distress from an apprehension of their sin and misery; or those who have been overcome with a sweet sense of the greatness, wonderfulness, and excellency of divine things" (J Edwards, *Distinguishing Marks*, p. 123). Of those who were manifesting, he observed that while some no doubt felt more able to do so because others were doing the same, he had detected very few who were feigning, while he had seen very many who had been so touched by God that it would have been "undoubtedly impossible for them to avoid" their manifestations (J Edwards, *Distinguishing Marks*, p. 124). Edwards also recognised the power of observed reactions. Those seeing bodily manifestations of extreme distress or abundant joy will have a much stronger grasp of what is felt than if they had merely heard "a dull narration of one which is inexperienced and insensible himself" (J Edwards, *Distinguishing Marks*, p. 99).

So what does it feel like when you fall under the power of God? I have examined my own experiences, which in some ways can have similarities to receiving a general anaesthetic and being told to count to ten. One two three, you begin counting and wondering whether the anaesthetic will fail to work. Four . . . five . . . seven or is it six, the anaesthetic begins to take a grip. And the next thing you know you are coming round, and it's all over. On some occasions it has seemed as if waves of love have begun, like an incoming tide, to wash against me. At first the impact is slight, as if from a distance. Gradually the impact intensifies until I have been overwhelmed with waves of divine love and the next thing I know I am gently falling to the floor. On other occasions the sensation has been more of a burning heat that steadily intensified, first at my fingertips and then all over my body. It felt like a revelation of just a small fraction of the power of God. The living flames of love enfolded me until once more I fell to the floor, captivated by the living Christ. Sometimes I have immediately rested peacefully on the floor. On other occasions I have been trembling or shaking, whether in my hand or all over. There is no standard response that we should try to reproduce. What matters is an openness to meet with God. Let the external manifestations take whatever course the Spirit chooses.

Drunkenness

The Bible reveals that the symptoms of an intense spiritual encounter can also have parallels with drunkenness. In the Old Testament, when Hannah was rapt in prayer, Eli the priest completely misread her fervour, and bluntly accused her of being drunk: "How long will you keep on getting drunk? Get rid of your wine" (1 Sam 1:14). Hannah's reply is as categorical as Eli's accusation: "I have not been drinking wine or beer; I was pouring out my soul to the Lord" (1 Sam 1:15).

When the Spirit was poured out at Pentecost, the disciples were so caught up in the Lord that their joy overflowed on to the streets. While some were amazed and intrigued, others immediately made fun of them: "They have had too much wine" (Acts 2:13). Peter took up this charge at the beginning of his message, as a way of explaining what had really taken place: "These men are not drunk, as you suppose. It's only nine in the morning! No, this is what was spoken by the prophet Joel" (Acts 2:15–16).

Many commentators have connected this accusation of drunkenness to their speaking in tongues. To be sure, hearing tongues for the first time can sound very strange to some ears. But Luke makes it plain that on this particular occasion the Spirit gave to the Apostles languages that were understood by the crowds. What intrigued and amazed the crowd was not unintelligible tongues but the fact that everyone could understand the Galileans in their various native languages (Acts 2:7–8). Such linguistic expertise would normally be taken as a sign of exceptional learning, not drunkenness. To be sure, it cannot be proved that the crowds saw physical symptoms usually associated with drunkenness, but we know the crowd saw such symptoms as these: a great deal of voluble enthusiasm; an abundance of joy, welling up in vigorous praise, whether spoken or in song. It is at least possible that they also saw people rapt in God, resting on the floor or even staggering, drunk with joy in the Lord.

The Apostle Paul picks up on the signs of apparent drunkenness in Ephesians 5:18: "Do not get drunk on wine, which leads to debauchery. Instead, be filled with the Spirit." Some interpret this as a straightforward contrast: wine makes people go out of control, while the Spirit brings self-control. But why should Paul use this particular contrast? Could it be that he knew and expected the churches to know what it is to be drunk with the Spirit of God? To be under the influence not of too much alcohol that leads to a surge of animal appetites and excess, but rather to be under the influence of the Holy Spirit, intoxicated with holy joy.

Certainly, the Spirit brings control of the sinful nature, but God's kind of self-control is very different to the dull religious conformity of Sunday-best respectability or a stiff upper lip. No stiff and starched legalism could ever conceivably be confused with drunkenness. If the worship of many traditional churches today had been taken out on to the streets at Pentecost, the crowds would not have accused them of drunkenness. They would have presumed they had just come from a funeral. Spirit-led self-control leads to behaviour and experiences that are completely outside the realm of both dry as dust religion and normal sobriety. Where we control the Spirit, there will be no release of God's abundant life. But where the Spirit controls us there are likely to be symptoms easily confused with drunkenness as we experience "inexpressible and glorious joy" (1 Pet 1:8).

In the recent outpouring I have seen some stagger and stumble as if drunk. Others lean on one another, strength sapped from their legs even as joy wells up in their spirit, overcome by God. Still others slip slowly down the wall on which they are leaning, or slide gradually off their seat and

on to the floor. For some, even their words have become
slurred, and their manner drowsy. On one occasion, the
moment I began to receive prayer I felt instantaneously
drunk. It's been over twenty years since I was drunk with
alcohol, but you remember the sensations, and in that
moment, drunk with the Spirit, I took a couple of uncertain
steps and fell to the floor. To be drunk on alcohol is to have
all sensations dulled, but to be drunk with the Spirit is to
have an intensified awareness of God. As I lay on the floor
I was intensely alert in mind and in Spirit, receiving from the
living God. Such symptoms of drunkenness are not an end in
themselves, but simply a way in which God overwhelms some
of us as a prelude, enabling us to concentrate on Christ alone.
Jeremiah plainly had just such an encounter with God:

> I am like a drunken man
> like a man overcome by wine,
> because of the LORD
> and his holy words.
>
> (Jer 23:9)

Shaking and trembling

Another frequent set of symptoms is shaking and trembling.
I have seen some believers tremble lightly whenever they
sense the power of God coming upon them. Others shake
with considerable force. Some shake for a while, then rest
peacefully before God. Others continue to tremble, shake
or shudder for some considerable time, whether remaining
upright or lying down. Occasionally, someone moves with
enormous vigour. Their arms may flap, their bodies jerk and
quiver. I recently saw one man begin to leap up and down
as if on a pogo stick, while those praying for him kept him
safely away from those already lying on the ground. After
several minutes he jumped himself horizontal on the carpet,
and as prayer for him was quietly continued, his back arched
and shuddered for a minute or two before he finally came

to rest. It was as if an enormous electric current had passed through him – a revelation and impartation of what Jesus called "power from on high" (Luke 24:49). How can we explain such strange responses, which are hardly the stuff of conventional church services? Above all, is there any biblical precedent?

Faced with situations of danger and fear, a typical and involuntary human reaction is to begin to shake. The Psalmist describes his own response to danger in such terms: "Fear and trembling have beset me" (Ps 55:5). Given this normal human reaction, it is hardly surprising that powerful encounters with the living God will sometimes provoke similar physical reactions. At Sinai, when there was thunder and lightning, the sound of a trumpet and the mountain was enveloped by thick cloud; the people were greatly moved by the sense of the presence of God, and without exception they were all trembling (Exod 19:16). When Moses descended the mountain, and there were further signs of God's presence, again the people "trembled with fear" (Exod 20:18). Twice in the New Testament reference is made to Moses himself trembling with fear before the presence of the Lord, before the burning bush (Acts 7:32) and at Mount Sinai (Heb 12:21). Many generations later, when the grave sins of Israel are unmasked, Ezra reports another widespread outbreak of trembling: "Everyone who trembled at the words of the God of Israel gathered round me because of this unfaithfulness of the exiles" (Ezra 9:4). In the New Testament, the woman who was healed of a haemorrhage by touching Jesus's cloak falls trembling at his feet when he asks who touched him (Luke 8:47). Similarly, when the prison doors in Philippi are miraculously opened, the jailor falls trembling before Paul and Silas, then urgently asks, "What must I do to be saved?" (Acts 16:29–30).

In the Old Testament, both Moses and David invite the nations to tremble before the Lord in his power (Exod 15:14; 1 Chr 16:30). The nations should tremble because the Lord reigns (Ps 99:1). When God moves in power, all who live in Israel will tremble (Joel 2:1), including the complacent and ungodly (Isa 32:11). In times of judgment, all kingdoms will tremble (Isa 23:11), the idols will tremble (Isa 19:1), the mountains will tremble (Nahum 1:5), even the earth and sky will tremble (Isa 13:13; Joel 3:16). Israel will return "with trembling to the LORD and his blessings in the last days" (Hosea 3:5, see also 11:10, 11). The Gentiles will also turn in great numbers to the living God, with fear and trembling (Mic 7:17).

The Psalmists not only speak of trembling before God, but also commend it. There is trembling due to fear of God (Ps 119:120), and trembling at his Word (Ps 119:161). All the earth is called to tremble at the presence of the Lord (Ps 114:7). As we worship God in the splendour of his holiness, trembling is a natural result or side-effect (Ps 99:1). Those who serve the Lord with fear, should also "rejoice with trembling" (Ps 2:11).

Several prophets give personal testimony to trembling before God. Isaiah speaks of trembling at God's Word (Isa 66:5). Jeremiah links trembling with his experience of spiritual drunkenness, for he also reports that, because of the Lord and his holy words, all his bones tremble (Jer 23:9). A trembling in the bones suggests that Jeremiah experienced not a light and delicate shivering but rather a bone-deep shaking in God's presence. Jeremiah also hears God commending such trembling as a natural and fitting response:

> "Should you not fear me?" declares the LORD,
> "Should you not tremble in my presence?"
> (Jer 5:22)

Daniel is another prophet who trembles before God. After he fell into a deep sleep and heard from God while resting on the ground, he is then touched by a hand. Rising to his hands and knees he begins to tremble on all fours. A voice from God speaks, calling him to his feet, and so he stands up, continuing to tremble before the Lord, as he awaits further revelation (Dan 10:10–11). In short, trembling in the Bible is a natural, spontaneous, and generally involuntary response to God's power, holiness, judgment, presence and Word.

Bizarre responses

If we are truly open to the Holy Spirit we cannot rule out responses that are even more strange than falling down, apparent drunkenness and shaking. Our upbringing and Christian experience will produce a gut reaction to bizarre manifestations. Some will be instinctively excited. Others will be just as immediately suspicious or even dismissive, cynical and hostile.

In order to discourage any preoccupation with the more exotic and off-beat phenomena, I don't propose to describe any that I have seen personally. Rather, I want to identify a few examples from the Old Testament. Moses lifting his staff before the Red Sea seems fairly strange behaviour (Exod 14). The modern Western mind might ask, "Why not simply pray, without the physical stuff?" But Moses obeyed God, and it actually worked. As to Joshua, the strategy for taking Jericho is hardly from the standard military textbook of the day, but when the trumpets sounded and the people shouted on the seventh circuit on the seventh day, the Lord gave them the city just as he had promised (Josh 6).

If these signs do not seem unduly strange, consider the bizarre obedience God required from the prophets. Isaiah walked stripped and barefoot for three years as a sign of the coming Assyrian defeat and humiliation of Egypt and Cush (Isa 20:2–5). Jeremiah smashed a pot in full public view as a sign of the disaster coming upon Jerusalem: "This is what the LORD Almighty says: I will smash this nation and this city just as this potter's jar is smashed and cannot be repaired" (Jer 19:11). Ezekiel gave public performance to a series of prophetic enactments. He packed his bags by day and left the city at dusk, using a hole he had dug through the city wall, as signs that the Jews would be taken into exile as captives. Then he trembled while eating and shuddered in fear as he drank, as signs of the anxiety and despair of the years of exile (Ezek 12:3–20).

In short, God has always called some believers to strange acts of obedience. Their bodies become prophetic symbols, with which they enact signs of God's words and works.

Even though such things are almost bound to make us feel uncomfortable and even quizzical, the Lord reserves the right to use his people in such ways. But we must take care to avoid majoring on minors. Both enthusiasts and detractors of the present work of God may be tempted to focus on the bizarre, but to do so will inevitably produce a gross distortion and caricature of the outpouring of the Holy Spirit.

We have looked carefully in this chapter at common physical manifestations that arise from powerful encounters with the living God. As Martyn Lloyd-Jones observed, in the light of his medical training: "Let us be very careful that we do not do violence to man's very nature and constitution. Man reacts as a whole. And it is just folly to expect that he can react in the realm of the spiritual without anything happening to the rest of him, to the soul, and to the body"(Lloyd-Jones, *Revival*, p. 145). When God pours out his Spirit we should be neither surprised nor threatened by strong feelings and vigorous physical reactions. King David gave a robust retort to Michal when she complained that his enthusiastic response to God was over the top and unbecoming:

I will celebrate before the LORD. I will become even more undignified than this . . .

(2 Sam 6:21-2)

Chapter 7

GETTING IT RIGHT

In the last two chapters we have explored the strong emotions and physical manifestations that accompany a powerful work of God. Previously we showed that similar phenomena accompanied the outpourings of the Great Awakening. But now we must face a burning question. How can we be sure that such experiences truly come from God?

Reasons for caution

Because the emotional and physical manifestations are so immediate and eye-catching, they are bound to seize the attention first. Some will naturally be inclined to point at them and declare, "These are sure and certain signs of a true work of God." I trust that by now it is obvious that I am committed to the signs; indeed I have experienced many of them and this book is designed in part to commend them. However, we need to insist carefully that just because we see certain outward manifestations, it does not in itself prove that the Holy Spirit is at work. We will consider five reasons for this necessary caution:

1) Manipulation
People could be manipulated by those leading a meeting. The reasons may vary. One may force his favoured response through love of power or fame. Another may pressure people to react in a specific way because in the past these particular manifestations have led to much genuine and lasting blessing.

Whether the leaders are unscrupulous or are acting out of misplaced and ill-considered zeal, we still need to face the fact that people can be worked up and forced to respond in a particular way. The presence of manifestations cannot in itself guarantee that leaders are behaving properly or that the Spirit is truly at work.

Charles Finney, who was all in favour of genuine manifestations as the natural accompaniment to true revival, considered it his duty to speak out against the spurious. On one occasion Finney visited a camp meeting in New York State where, after several sermons and much exhortation, prayer and singing, there was still little or no visible excitement. Several of the leaders consulted together and then one of the most energetic came down from the platform and stood in front of a row of women. He began to clap his hands with great vigour while bellowing at the top of his voice, "Power! Power!! Power!!!" The fervour spread, as one after another began to clap, shout, shriek and fall to the ground. The platform party then proclaimed that the power of God was revealed from heaven, and left the meeting much gratified. Finney's critique is justly severe: "In the getting up of this excitement there was not a word of truth communicated; there was no prayer or exhortation – nothing but a most vociferous shouting . . . So far as such efforts to promote revivals are made, they are undoubtedly highly disastrous, and should be entirely discouraged" (Finney, *Reflections on Revival*, pp. 50–1). Of course, in such denunciation we always have to be scrupulously careful not to speak out against a genuine work of God. When the Spirit truly comes there will also be powerful reactions, but there need be no mindless pressuring of the people.

2) Mass hysteria
The emotional temperature of a meeting may become so intense that people become caught up in a common response, carried away in the heat of the moment. This factor of a crowd's collective reaction needs to be faced honestly, and leaders need to be ready to dampen down fires of excitement should they begin to burn too vigorously, and

rage like wildfire. However, this possibility cannot be used to explain away every single example of such phenomena. In Toronto, where the manifestations were many and powerful, I observed that they were also extremely diverse. What is more, people were able to disengage quite freely, standing at the side of the meeting to observe or stepping outside for a cup of coffee. There was no evidence of anyone being whipped up or compelled into some kind of hysterical frenzy. Nonetheless, we have to acknowledge that mass hysteria remains a possible explanation for some phenomena.

3) Deliberate imitation
Mass hysteria is about being carried away unconsciously by emotional peer pressure. A third explanation for the manifestations is that some people choose outward conformity quite deliberately, copying others. Some may be attention-seeking. Whether needy or self-indulgent, they crave all eyes resting upon them. Charles Wesley developed a policy of ignoring them if they were quiet and having them ejected if they were noisy.

Others may have misunderstood the significance of external manifestations. Some think that bodily responses are medals of spiritual advancement, and so imitate the reactions of others to attempt to elevate their own spiritual standing. Still others confuse the priority of meeting God with the bodily side-effects. They assume that physical reactions are a prerequisite to meeting with God, a means to that end rather than a secondary consequence.

This confusion should not be found surprising. I remember one church leader telling me how he was converted the night before his baptism. He'd asked to be baptised in the misguided hope that the external rite would save him. He awoke that Saturday night realising the folly of his actions and surrendered his life to Christ. The next day his baptism was no longer an empty ritual of external conformity, but had become a wonderful celebration of saving faith. If people get confused about familiar things, like communion and baptism, it is hardly surprising if some get confused about unusual emotional and physical manifestations in a time of spiritual refreshing.

4) Satanic counterfeit

Satan is the great deceiver. The one who masquerades as an angel of light (2 Cor 11:14) will also seek to parody the works of the Spirit of God, even as Pharaoh's magicians attempted to imitate and match the signs God gave to Moses and Aaron (Exod 7:10–12). We need to face the reality of satanic counterfeit without slipping into paranoia and fear. We can take great comfort from the outcome of the confrontation between Aaron's rod and those of the Egyptian sorcerers: while the Egyptians could match Aaron in turning their staffs into snakes, their staffs were swallowed up by Aaron's. Our God is mightier! To attribute every manifestation to Satan is absurd, but to exclude the possibility that some could have a demonic origin is naive.

It is very curious, even perverse, that some Christians find it easy to detect Satan behind all dramatic phenomena and struggle with the thought that God could manifest his powerful presence in such ways. It is as if they have a higher view of Satan's capacity to intervene than Christ's. Sometimes they have unconsciously embraced non-interventionist assumptions for how God relates to the world today. This is really a form of deism, an old enemy of the Christian doctrine of God. Sometimes they are limiting God either through a rigid dispensationalist model, or by excluding the possibility that the living God could work in ways that exceed their own experiences. The truth is that such sceptics are ignorant of both the Bible and the history of revivals.

5) The Bible's silence

We come to our final reason for suggesting that external manifestations cannot in themselves prove that the Holy Spirit is at work. Quite simply there is no list in the New Testament of utterly reliable physical or emotional signs. We are never told that certain physical reactions are compulsory. Nor are we told that their presence can be taken in itself as a cast-iron guarantee for a work of God. Scripture does not give us grounds to be able to prove conclusively that the Holy Spirit is being poured out, simply by pointing to the evidence of emotional and physical manifestations.

Beyond hesitancy

Just as some want the manifestations to mean more than they do in order to commend a work of God, others try to exploit them to justify the opposite intent. For the opponents and sceptics, the very presence of the signs seems sufficient warrant to write off a church or movement. We therefore insist that the mere presence of such emotional and physical reactions cannot reasonably justify the conclusion that God cannot possibly be at work.

1) Biblical precedent

While Scripture does not allow us to suggest that these phenomena automatically guarantee that God is at work, it is equally true that nowhere does Scripture exclude these manifestations. Indeed, as we have seen in earlier chapters, dramatic encounters with God, strong emotional responses, crying out with tears and with joy, the appearance of drunkenness, trembling, and falling down are all found in the Bible. Anyone who suggests that such reactions prove God cannot be at work is either ignorant of Scripture or unable to see the evidence on the written page, blinded by their own prejudice.

2) The witness of history

To be sure, such manifestations can be disturbing, for they are often both strange and vigorous. Nonetheless, news of unfamiliar behaviour or strength of feeling cannot be a sufficient reason to exclude the possibility that God may be at work. To the witness of Scripture we have added the witness of the Great Awakening, and could readily have continued the study through many subsequent revivals. Sometimes the main reason we are cautious about the legitimacy or plausibility of such manifestations is that modern evangelical Christians have become deeply ignorant of their own heritage, particularly the history of revivals and the attendant phenomena.

3) Respectable religion

In the Great Awakening, the revivalists were quickly denounced as enthusiasts, accused of whipping up their congregations into a seething ferment. One group of North American church leaders complained in these terms about George Whitefield and his colleagues in 1741:

> Their preaching the terrors of the law . . . and so indus-triously working on the passions and affections of weak minds, as to cause them to cry out in a hideous manner, and fall down in convulsion-like fits, to the marring of the profiting both of themselves and others . . . and then, after all, boasting of these things as the work of God, which we are persuaded do proceed from an inferior or worse cause. (Tracy, *The Great Awakening*, pp. 71–2)

In their very nature, vigorous emotional and physical reactions rapidly become an outrage to respectable religion. Where Christianity has been reduced from a living faith to a social custom, nothing is more shocking than an outbreak of holy fire.

4) Mind-centred religion

The manifestations are also an affront to cerebral religion. Biblical Christianity can degenerate into a philosophical system, an abstract construct of doctrines confined to the intellectual plane. Evangelicalism is not exempt from the possibility of this tyranny of the mind. One of the many clergy converted under George Whitefield's preaching explained how his faith had been previously merely theoretical: "I have been a scholar, and have preached the doctrines of grace for a long time, but I believe I have never felt the power of them in my soul" (Tracy, *The Great Awakening*, p. 103).

Just as anti-intellectualism is a vice, for reason is one of

God's great gifts to men and women, cerebral religion is an equal vice. The person who is gripped by cerebral religion is only able to receive what their mind can accept and fully comprehend. They limit God to operating only within the confines of their own intellectual grasp and system. They sneer with intellectual arrogance at the benighted fools who speak of experiences of God, forgetting that Christ commended child-like faith.

Those for whom Christian faith is dominated by the mind are always affronted by responses to God, whether emotional or physical, that defy analysis and comprehension. Our faith is reasonable – it makes sense. But Christian faith is not rationalistic, circumscribed by human reason, for our God transcends the capacities of the human mind. If I wait until I understand fully before I receive, I will never understand enough to receive all that God longs to give me. But if I learn to receive willingly and humbly from the presence of God, then the Spirit himself will assist me in reflecting on what I have received. The mind is a great servant of true religion, but where the mind has mastery over our response to God, the free flow of the Spirit will be fatally restricted.

Blaise Pascal, the renowned French mathematician and physicist, prepared in his *Pensées* a brilliant and original reasoned defence of Christian convictions. But he never confused the reasonings of his own finite mind with the reality of the living God. On 23 November 1654, he experienced personal revival in a power encounter with the Holy Spirit. He wrote a description of this experience on to a piece of parchment which he then carried with him, sewn into his clothing, for the rest of his life. A brief extract conveys the intensity of this encounter with the manifest presence of God. The sharpest of intellects is no reason to exclude oneself from the fires of revival:

Fire
God of Abraham, God of Isaac, God of Jacob,
not of philosophers and scholars.
Certainty, certainty, heartfelt, joy, peace.
God of Jesus Christ.

God of Jesus Christ.
My God and your God.
Thy God shall be my God.
The world forgotten, and everything except God.
He can only be found by the ways taught in the
    Gospels.
Greatness of the human soul.
O righteous Father, the world had not known thee,
but I have known thee.
Joy, joy, joy, tears of joy . . .

5) *Keeping control*

A religion governed by the priority of control has little
stomach for these signs. The control may be cultural –
the stiff upper lip of traditional English Christianity. The
control may be in the hands of an individual or a power
block, dominating the life and development of a local church.
David Watson used to describe a church building with every
window closed and papers piled up neatly. When the windows
are opened, the Spirit of God breathes life into the room, with
the side-effect that the neat piles of paper are sent flying.
Finally someone decides that for the sake of neatness the
windows must be shut. The piles of paper return to their
pristine condition, but the Spirit is no longer permitted to
blow freely. The order to which churches often cling comes
not from heaven, but the graveyard.

A religion of control hates unpredictability. It wants everything planned, organised and explained. Of course, we don't
have to swing to the opposite extreme. The Spirit does indeed
work through good planning and preparation. But those
committed to control cannot conceive of the Spirit working
spontaneously. They hate the unexpected, and hide behind
the instruction of the Apostle Paul: "everything should be
done in a fitting and orderly way" (1 Cor 14:40). For many
churches, decent order entails business as usual, Sunday after
dreary Sunday. Nothing ever changes, the same people lead,
preach and pray, with the same totally predictable results,
as it was in the beginning, is now and shall be for ever.
Charismatic churches sometimes serve up a more modern

menu while suffering from the same crisis of control and predictability.

The stumbling block is found in our concept of decent order, which is very often radically different from that held by the first Christians. For Paul, decent order included different people bringing hymns, words of instruction, revelations; three people taking it in turns to speak in tongues, three interpretations, two or three prophecies; and the possibility that an unbeliever might drop in, hear a prophecy, then fall down and worship, declaring, "God is really among you!" (1 Cor 14). From elsewhere in the New Testament we can add to this heady cocktail the possibilities of prayer for healing and deliverance, which could lead to cries of joy or demonic shrieking (Acts 3:8, 8:7–8). All too easily we redefine the phrase "decent order" in the light of our own attenuated experiences and expectations.

A clear understanding of what the Bible means by decent order will shatter the bonds of controlled religion, making space for the dramatic eventfulness of the Holy Spirit. Where the Spirit is Lord, there is freedom, and a dynamic, biblical concept of order is released into the Church. To the devotees of human control, such vitality is always threatening and distressing. Unless God breaks through their defensive barriers, they will resist the dynamic of heavenly order with all their might.

Signs will follow

So far in this chapter we have argued for two propositions held in tension. On the one hand, the presence of manifestations cannot prove that God is at work. On the other, their presence certainly cannot prove that God is not at work. The witness of both the Bible and subsequent revivals requires us to add a third proposition. When God is pouring out his Spirit in power it is only reasonable to expect an increase in such manifestations. They will not be the main event, the heart of what is going on. But as side-effects their eruption is practically inevitable, as a result of our whole being responding to the powerful presence of God. The manifestations should not be our focus of attention, but those who know their Bible and church history should react to the manifestations neither with surprise, as if they were unexpected, nor with resistance, as if they were a threat. They come as a natural and welcome bonus when God pours out his Spirit upon a thirsty church.

Learning from excess

No sooner do we speak of the manifestations as welcome and natural than we need to recognise ways in which they can be misused. The true friend of a work of God, rather than deny the possibility of error, is always ready to deal with it. The outpouring of the Holy Spirit is so precious that it needs wise handling.

1) Over-emphasis on manifestations

As we have already argued, the manifestations are secondary, for what matters far more is a deep and life-changing encounter with God. The opponents of an outpouring and those who go over the top have more in common than they usually realise. They are the twin errors of phenomeno-centricity, for both extremes major on minors, making too much of emotional and physical reactions. It seems this pair of excesses are both inevitable. There will always be some who go over the top with the manifestations and others who reject them wholesale and out of hand.

2) Manifestations in the flesh

We have dealt with this excess already. Whether through pretence or manipulation, some will abuse the manifestations for their own ends. We have to face a simple truth: some manifestations will inevitably occur not through the Spirit of God but in the flesh. There will always be tares. But this is not only true of dramatic manifestations. According to Jesus's parables of the field of wheat and tares (Matt 13:24–30, 36–43) and the catch of good and bad fish (Matt 13:47–50), every church will know a mixed harvest. It would be absurd to expect the manifestations to be totally free from the tares that characterise every other aspect of Christian living.

3) Pride

There is no aspect of human ability and experience that cannot become fodder to our pride. Just as Christians can suffer from pride in their denominational label, or pride in their spiritual gifts, some will be tempted to take pride in their manifestations and make too much of them: whether they have laughed, whether they have fallen down, and so on. Pride feeds on anything that distinguishes us from one another, and so some are bound either to carry airs of self-importance or even to make an explicit claim to spiritual superiority. Such puffed up nonsense needs deflating as soon as possible. Our only justification before God is found neither in our character nor our accomplishments, neither in our denomination nor our gifts, but only in the righteousness of Christ. In Christ we are justified, and in him every believer's status is equal.

Others will probably confuse blessing with arrival. They may briefly suppose that they have received the ultimate empowerment, so that now they have nothing more to receive from God. They will be tempted to announce to others that once they have entered this experience, Christian living and the conversion of the world will be so easy as to be effortless. It will not take long for their fond illusions to be dashed. Those who have been truly touched by God will have a very different reaction. As one said to me, "God touched me yesterday and now I desire to be filled again. My past blessing doesn't make me take God for granted, it makes me more thirsty and needy today." The touch of God is like manna in the wilderness: every day we need to come afresh, dependent on God once again (Exod 16:19–20). If we try to live on past closeness to God, the experience will turn to dust in our hands.

Others will almost certainly fall into the old trap of claiming sinless perfection, presuming that having received a fresh touch of God's love they have now left their sinful nature behind once for all. The plain teaching of Scripture and the clear witness of church history is that all who think they are free from sin in this life suffer a terrible delusion (1 John 1:8). At best they are self-deluded, at worst they deceive others while secretly knowing the continuing presence of indwelling sin. Sinless perfection will never be the direct result of conversion, nor of being filled with the Spirit, nor certainly through weeping or laughing, falling or shaking. Such idle hopes are sustained only by folly or pride. There is only one way for any Christian to be totally freed from their sinful nature, and that is death.

4) Speculative theories

When we are faced with a sudden increase in manifestations it is only natural to try to make as much sense of them as we can. But it becomes all too easy to overstep the mark. Apart from describing many and diverse manifestations, the Bible gives us very little information. What is more, it is very difficult to generalise from our own experience or observations. We really do not know whether a certain type of person and a certain type of manifestation tend to go together. We really do not know whether similar symptoms in different people indicate a similar kind of meeting with God. If the same person has a similar reaction on different occasions we really cannot tell what is going on within them. We really do not know whether the symptoms are loosely connected to what God is doing or whether they offer a more precise indication. In short, we have a natural desire to understand, explain and interpret, but a veil of obscurity is drawn across the meaning and status of the various manifestations.

While some readily accept the limits of human under-standing, for others there is an irresistible attraction to the mysterious significance of different manifestations. I have come across three kinds of speculation. Firstly, some attempt to determine a universal sequence of responses, mapping out an order from their own experience and then imposing this on others, advising them that their responses should automatically follow the same course. There's nothing wrong with analysing our personal pattern of response – for example, first I fell down quietly, then I laughed, then I twitched, then I shook violently and fell quietly, then I shook and fell and continued to shake. But there is really no justification for turning this into a universal theory, and saying that others must necessarily and always experience manifestations in the same order.

If some concentrate on a sequence of manifestations, others are tempted to delineate a hierarchy of response. For example, to stand quietly to receive is good, to fall quietly is better, but to leap around like a mannequin on speed really is the Everest of manifestations. Those with the opposite prejudices will naturally want to reverse this presumed hierarchy, claiming that the quieter the response, the higher and more profound the inner work of God must surely be. Despite the attraction of being able to make sense and order out of the manifestations, there is no evidence to suggest we have enough hard information to even think of going down such a route.

The third kind of speculative theory treats the various responses as symbols. To be sure, some people's response is indeed symbolic. But the attraction of a universal theory of manifestations is the possibility of constructing a code-breakers' book, so that those ministering can infallibly interpret every conceivable physical response. The bottom line is that this cannot be done. We do not have the expertise and the Bible gives no encouragement to pursue such a line of enquiry.

Often we would like things to be thoroughly watertight and defined. The gullible may be drawn to a universal theory of manifestations, whether it claims to organise them in a sequence or hierarchy, or presumes to crack their symbolic code. Such speculation is riddled with imprecision and depends more on guesswork than knowledge. This is one line of enquiry that needs to be approached with great caution, since it is likely to prove nothing more than a dead end. We need to concentrate on receiving from God and meeting with God, not tabulating and systematising the resultant manifestations. No one can codify and fully define the outpouring of living waters. The sovereign work of God is always shrouded in mystery, too high for any of us to comprehend fully.

5) Attempts to monopolise

Historical accounts of a period of renewal or revival will naturally result in the tracing of a kind of spiritual family tree: who prayed for whom, and how the movement spread. Such an approach may mislead us into looking for a pivotal individual who makes everything happen. If we really believe in an all-powerful God, then we need to stress that while it is perfectly possible and appropriate to trace such links, in the final analysis we are dealing not with a work of man but of God.

I have always been hesitant about the frequent references in the Christian press to the "Toronto blessing" and the "Toronto phenomena" for exactly this reason. I want to stress emphatically that I saw no attempt whatsoever at the Airport Vineyard to monopolise the move of God in this way. Their leaders were at great pains every night to stress that this is not a work of their church, nor a work of the Vineyard network. Such journalistic slogans may be inevitable, but they seem dishonouring to the Spirit of God. To be sure, we need the humility to say that this little, previously insignificant church in Toronto has become a starting point for a fresh wave of the Spirit. But at the same time we need to be clear that this is a work of God, not of men. We are not replicating the Airport Vineyard experience, neither are they providing franchise operations in revival. What God has poured out upon their church they are now seeking to give away as quickly as they can, with no strings attached. So far as I could see, the last thing anyone in Toronto wants is to attempt to monopolise the blessing. That would surely bring dishonour to God and result in the quenching of the Spirit.

This danger seems to have arisen in the past in two ways. Firstly, an over-ambitious leader may be tempted to lay claim to a move of God, presenting himself as the only true source and fountainhead. Secondly, those who count themselves greatly blessed by a particular leader may begin, out of loyalty and appreciation, to trumpet his cause above all others. The history of the division between John Wesley and George Whitefield actually took place on two levels. Their public dispute was theological, specifically over Arminian and

Calvinistic doctrines of free will and the sovereignty of God. However, behind the scenes there was a rivalry among some of their supporters that was almost tribal, something like the rivalry between fans of different football teams. Neither Wesley nor Whitefield attempted to monopolise the blessing and lay claim to sole pre-eminence. I suspect however that some of their followers were less scrupulous and reluctant. I have sometimes encountered similar enthusiasm among devoted followers of contemporary Christian leaders, but discretion suggests it would not be wise or helpful to name any names! Nonetheless, the warning is clear. When God begins to move in power there is a natural temptation for someone to attempt to monopolise the blessing.

6) Illuminism

The dangers of illuminism have always dogged the Church. The early Christians had to deal with the threat of gnosticism, which claimed that a higher knowledge was only available to its initiates. At the Reformation, Luther quickly had to do battle with those who wanted not only to reform the Church, but to abolish all creeds, learning and even the Scriptures. "Why bother with such things," they asked, "when you have received the inner light?"

At the time of the Great Awakening the same hazards arose. At the fringes of a revival there will always be crazy extremes, as there have been during the last thirty years of charismatic renewal. For example, Charles Wesley held an interview with a self-styled prophetess who was winning an enthusiastic following among the early Methodists. When asked a question she would begin groaning and then declaimed her reply in an unnatural voice, like a Grecian oracle. She lavished praise on those most devoted to her and insisted on her own divine inspiration. When Wesley refused to accept her spiritual authority she "cried that the devil was in me, that I was a fool, a blockhead, a blind leader of the blind set to put out the people's eyes". Charles recognised the vital necessity of promptly excluding her from their meetings.

Turning back to the major aberrations, an extreme and exclusive dependence on intuitive impressions has several likely consequences. Firstly, the Bible will be demoted to a secondary position, neglected or even despised. Jim Jones, who led a cult whose members eventually committed mass suicide, was said to have thrown a Bible to the floor, demanding that his followers should no longer bother with the book when he could provide direct and higher revelation. Illuminists never want their fresh-minted revelations tested at the bar of Scripture. Secondly, biblical morality will almost certainly be abandoned – several such groups have concluded over the centuries that polygamy should make a come-back. Thirdly, doctrines will steadily drift away from biblical ortho-doxy. Fourthly, the leading illuminists will exert tremendous power over gullible followers, who, like nestlings straining to be fed with beaks stretched wide, eagerly await the next batch of fresh revelations. Illuminism leads to domination of the weak.

7) A package deal
When we see the Spirit moving in power it is always tempting to use the phenomena as proofs or guarantors of unrelated teaching. For example, I was converted in an Anglican church but now practise believers' baptism. To pray for God to come in power upon someone being baptised, and upon the congregation, is entirely honouring to God. But God would surely be dishonoured if I then declared that the manifest presence of the Spirit proved and vindicated our baptismal practice and demonstrated conclusively that infant baptisers are wrong. To do so would be to introduce a needlessly divisive and controversial note. It would be an abuse of spiritual authority.

Some may offer a package deal not linked to a debated practice but to a false teaching. Their argument runs that, because the Spirit is clearly at work in their meetings, all that they teach must undoubtedly be correct and approved by God. Some who see God move in healing power also teach guaranteed material prosperity for every believer. I happen to think that this is dangerous nonsense for three reasons. First, the Bible suggests that God is more interested in helping us to give our money away than to get rich quick. Second, there are more Christians today in the developing world than in the West, and for many millions of them great material wealth is a non-starter. Third, for Christians in the West, our greatest need is not to ask God to bless our materialistic conformity, but to ask to be delivered from it, receiving in its place a fresh outpouring of spiritual riches. Never before has a church been so materially blessed as the Church in the West, and rarely has the Church been so spiritually impoverished.

Others will lay claim to the manifestations during a period of doctrinal controversy. When the debate over free will and predestination began to rage, John Wesley prayed in public meetings that the Spirit would vindicate his teaching, over against the Calvinists, by signs of witness. As his journal records, "Immediately one, and another, and another sunk to the earth: they dropped on every side as thunderstruck" (J Wesley, *Journal*, 23 April 1739). At this point Wesley was surely acting unwisely, offering a package deal to the crowd gathered to hear him. Several objections must be made to such a course of action. It was divisive, bringing doctrinal controversy to the fore in public meetings. It was inconclusive, for as we have already argued, the manifestations do not in themselves prove the work of the Spirit. Indeed, in a period of public controversy, the keenest supporters of a preacher might be tempted to fall to the ground simply to support the cause. It was misleading, because such manifestations were also seen in the Calvinists' meetings. It was inappropriate, because the correct place to thrash out a complex doctrinal disagreement between prominent leaders must be in private. In short, it was unwise. Such is the amazing power with which God is seen to work in times of refreshing and revival that even the finest of Christian leaders may try to make dramatic phenomena prove too much. Authentic manifestations are the side-effects of a meeting with God. They should never be exploited to press upon the people a package deal.

8) Quantity and quality

When the spiritual temperature hots up in a church it is all too easy to confuse quantity with quality. Some receive from God with vigorous manifestations on a regular basis and the impact on their lives is dramatic. The more they receive, the more they grow. Indeed, some grow so fast that their progress is positively breathtaking. What would take years of teaching, discipling and counselling, the Lord is capable of achieving in moments by the power of his Spirit. Others, however, show similar initial manifestations but make much less lasting progress and show little fruit.

I have prayed for some who have shown no immediate, outward evidence of the Spirit's outpouring, but the impact has still been immense. We knew just how acute Paula's needs were, and so Claire and I both felt disappointed after praying for her because we had seen no immediate evidence of the healing touch of Christ. The next day she phoned Claire to say the prayer ministry had been wonderful. She had received fresh hope from God and please could we pray with her some more. I also think of Steve – two weeks after receiving prayer, when nothing much had seemed to happen, he leaped to his feet to declare that, following several lean years spiritually, he had begun to devour the Bible at every opportunity and had a wonderful new awareness of the presence of God at home and at work.

On the other hand, I have also seen some receive prayer with no manifestations who have in truth received very little. One man saw himself as a defiant test case, out to prove that he would not fall over, come what may. He so closed his life to God that he received exactly what he wanted and nothing more: he stayed upright and he also stayed dry. Others have come for prayer surrounded by strong defensive walls, like a medieval castle. These may be theological hang-ups, barriers against expressing emotion, or even defences of self-protection to cope with deep hurt or rejection. For some, the Lord smashes right through those walls with one prayer and the impact is obvious and immense. For others there is a more prolonged work, soaking in prayer as the many layers of defence and resistance are gradually undermined and removed.

Jonathan Edwards's experiences were similar. He found that some had a very limited response, which in a day or two came to nothing. Others were deeply impressed, and their new convictions took deep root. Still others made a dramatic response at first which seemed to come to nothing, but later they were "seized with abiding convictions, and their affections became durable" (J Edwards, *The Revival In Northampton*, pp. 150–1). In short, you never can tell how much fruit will follow in a particular individual, nor can you afford to jump to hasty conclusions.

Some that have had very great raptures of joy . . . and have had their bodies overcome, and that very often, have manifested far less of the temper of Christians in their conduct since than some others that have been still and have made no great outward show. But then again, there are many others that have had extraordinary joys and emotions of mind, with frequent great effects upon their bodies, that behave themselves steadfastly, as humble, amiable, eminent Christians. (J Edwards, *The Revival in Northampton*, p. 159)

The truth is that there seems to be no direct correlation between quantity and quality. To be sure, we encourage people to receive everything that God has for them, with open and expectant hearts. What is more, as we open our lives more readily to God, the manifestations seem more likely to occur and even increase. My own tentative suggestion is that the manifestations appear to be more than secondary side-effects. They seem to serve as a bridge between the infinite and the finite, the bodily means by which the Lord mediates and applies supernatural resources of love and power to our inner being. Nonetheless, we must be careful to avoid the suggestion that we can judge with confidence and precision whether someone has been touched lightly or powerfully on the solitary basis of their immediate external symptoms. The quality and depth of what the Spirit has been doing can only be measured by lasting fruit, not merely by the immediate manifestations.

Chapter 8

FINDING IT HARD TO RECEIVE

We turn in this chapter to a different kind of excess, that of receiving too little. There is nothing more sad than to see a Christian who finds it hard to receive. Some find it much easier to believe that someone else will be blessed. They may even offer to pray for others. But as for themselves, it always seems so very hard to receive. In public meetings and personal ministry I have come across many reasons for this impasse. To make progress, the reasons for the blockage need to be found.

Some are held back by low self-esteem
Their explanation appears to be modest, but is actually a man-made trap: "I don't deserve to receive." Others suffer from a lack of assurance, sometimes tied to guilt: "Does God really accept me?" For those trapped in such ways the gospel of grace brings renewed hope by pointing to the death of Christ, crucified out of love for each and every individual. No matter how badly we feel about ourselves, no matter how guilty we judge ourselves to be, the Holy Spirit longs to bring more of the personal, saving love of Christ to our hearts.

Some are much too self-conscious
They are frightened to receive prayer because of a gnawing anxiety: "How will I react? Will I make a fool of myself?" Others, and this includes a number of ministers, are boxed in by fear of others: "How will *they* react to my response?" We need to learn to look to God and seek to please God alone, forgetting ourselves and breaking free from fear of

the opinions of others. As the proverb warns, "Fear of man will prove to be a snare, but whoever trusts in the LORD is kept safe" (Prov 29:25).

Some are trapped by the fear of superficial conformity
They concentrate so hard on not fitting in with the reactions of others that they close themselves off and end up not receiving much at all. We need to relax, learning to trust those praying for us, and above all to trust our Father God. Jesus provided reassurance that is strong and specific: "If you then, though you are evil, know how to give good gifts to your children, how much more will your Father in heaven give the Holy Spirit to those who ask him!" (Luke 11:13)

Fear of the supernatural makes some withdraw
"It's too powerful and threatening to me. I want to stay in control." Fear of the Lord is a natural response. It is perfectly reasonable to feel thoroughly daunted by the presence of God in awesome power. The dilemma is how to move beyond this initial apprehensiveness. The biblical solution is not to back off but to acknowledge our fear openly before God and then to request prayer for the peace that passes understanding.

Some want a "delete as applicable" spirituality
They would like to be able to indicate in advance which manifestations or spiritual gifts they will decline to accept. At one time I had this kind of hang-up about both the gift of tongues and also resting in the Spirit. It boils down to the issue of who is really Lord in my life. As if we have any right to parcel up a rejected gift of God and mark it "Return to Sender"! The only thing to do with such an arrogant attitude is to repent.

Some are held back by sin or the occult
It is quite ludicrous to ask for God's blessing if we are involved in major rebellion, holding on to unconfessed sin or satanic involvement. One woman came for prayer who was involved in an adulterous relationship: the only possible

first step towards spiritual blessing was to repent and break off the affair. A couple felt they were not getting anywhere as Christians, and then we discovered they had a collection of Tarot cards, ouija boards and other such occult artefacts. If they really wanted to make progress with God, they needed a bonfire of these vanities.

Some seek prayer but are holding on to deep and unresolved hurts

We have seen this with blocked bereavements, where the loss has been repressed, and also with victims of abuse, who have hidden the horror deep within. For as long as the hurt is locked up inside they are unable to open themselves to the Holy Spirit. Only when the pain is acknowledged and faced can they allow the Spirit of God to flood their lives with the balm of heavenly love. For some this prepares them for counselling ministry. For others this results in immediate emotional release. When the Holy Spirit is poured out in great power there is often a remarkable acceleration of emotional healing. Some needs that would take weeks of gentle treatment with counselling are dealt with in a single meeting under the supernatural love therapy of the Spirit of God.

Others have suffered from emotional neglect as children, with parents who either did not love them or failed to express love in ways their child could understand and receive. Such people's hearts can become like a fortress: defensive walls have been steadily reinforced to hide the pain and protect them from being hurt any more. The love of God releases the repressed emotion and lays siege to the defences. The only way to receive is to let the defences down, even though they have been built up during a lifetime of self-protection.

Some suffer from a fear of emotions

This hang-up, ironically, can often be very emotional. As we saw earlier, some deeply distrust everything except the rational processes, as if emotions are always more susceptible to the devil than to God. We can become so frightened of emotionalism that we treat every expression of emotion as suspect or wrong. Some Christians with a great intellectual grasp of the gospel have become emotionally stunted, crippled by their own fear, unable either to receive or express the joy of the Lord.

Some are dogged by the fear of past malpractice or a spiritual failure
They have come across excesses in the past and have come to equate manifestations with spiritual or psychological abuse. They may have seen someone fall over as a result of being pushed, who was left upset or even distraught. Or they may have seen someone fall over with no positive lasting fruit. Others may have been prayed for in the past, with no lasting results, so they are tempted to dismiss all such ministry and manifestations: "It doesn't work for me."

As a result, they have become deeply sceptical about any such manifestations. Their knee-jerk reaction is hostile, suspicious or dismissive. They tend to assume, sometimes unconsciously, that openness to God or any manifestations will inevitably lead to excess. This represents a confusion of symptoms with the cause that has triggered them. The manifestations are symptoms, but we have already recognised that a variety of causes can result in the same symptoms. Such attitudes reveal that someone is generalising too much from their own limited experience. We need to sympathise with those who have encountered abuses in the past, but at the same time we must urge them not to over-react. They need to look again at the Bible and also at Christian history, particularly revivals. As has often been said, the correct response to misuse is not disuse but right use.

The Thessalonian church had been burned by false prophecy about the second coming. As a result, they were fighting shy of any prophetic words, not wanting to get caught again. While Paul understood their caution, he made it plain that their exclusion of prophecy was unacceptable behaviour (1 Thess 5:19–20). Of course they had a responsibility to test all things in order to sort the genuine from the spurious. But then they also needed to ensure that they really were holding on to the good. To treat prophecy with contempt, Paul warned, is to put out the fire of the Spirit. Those who refuse to concede the possibility that God is at work when there are manifestations today are just as much at risk of treating God's works with contempt and putting out the Spirit's fire. To draw the conclusion that the kinds of manifestations we have discussed in this book can only have an ungodly origin is neither biblical, nor logical, nor defensible. Having tested all things we, just as much as the Thessalonians, have an absolute duty to hold on to all that is good.

Some are reluctant to receive love

They may have been taken advantage of in the name of love, and now they find it hard to receive the real thing. Others have been trained to have a stiff upper lip, whether through home, school or work. The example of Jesus surely demonstrates that to receive the love of Father God is by no means a sign of weakness and inadequacy but rather a sign of true strength. Real men are not emotion-free, self-sufficient and self-made. True humanity involves learning how to receive readily and repeatedly the abundant love of God.

Some have an inability to admit personal need

They may have been trained to be strong at all times and have become driven by a fear of failure or any hint of inadequacy. Others never acknowledge their own needs but reveal them indirectly by their need to be needed. They are always offering to help others, but they exact a high price. Instead of helping others to stand on their own feet they thrive on someone saying, "I don't know how I would cope without you." They like to take over, cultivating a continuing dependency. I think it was C S Lewis who once described such a person: "She always lived for others. You could tell the others she lived for by the hunted look in their eyes!" To admit need of God is hardly a sign of weakness. It is a sign of strength. As a car needs fuel and a baby needs its mother's milk, the Christian believer is designed to require love and power from on high. The beginning of renewal, refreshing and revival is to admit personal need.

Some are trapped by the limitations of their own experience
They become like a blind man, adamantly refusing to believe that others can see. For some this takes the form of pride: "I need no more than I have already received." This is the height of complacent folly. Which of us can truly say we have received everything God has to give or that we live fully and constantly in personal revival? Even the Apostle Paul insisted that he still had a long way to go: "Not that I have already obtained all this, or have already been made perfect, but I press on to take hold of that for which Christ Jesus took hold of me." (Phil 3:12) For the Spirit-filled believer there is no arrival in this life. There is always more to discover and receive.

Others struggle with the unfamiliar
The cry goes up: "It's just not what I'm used to." Jonathan Edwards found that this was a particular problem for some elderly believers. His own reply was to point to the day of Pentecost. From the very beginning of the Christian Church, whenever the Holy Spirit comes in power the impact is almost inevitably unfamiliar and unexpected (J Edwards, *Distinguishing Marks*, p. 90). We need to recognise that many elderly believers have prayed for years for revival in the Church. In the twentieth century they represent the generations of the faithful remnant, who stood firm in the faith faced with the onslaught of liberalism and a massive decline in church attendance in the western world. With patience, appreciation and graciousness we need to point such believers both to the Bible and to the history of revivals. We long that no one's expectations of what God can do will remain shackled within the confines of Christian experience in this century – barren of revival for so very long.

A third group are the victims of false teaching, which excludes the possibility of the Spirit coming in revival power upon the Church. Martyn Lloyd-Jones never shrank from denouncing this error which robs the Church of a thirst for genuine revival:

Does our doctrine of the Holy Spirit, and his work, leave

any room for revival either in the individual or in the church . . .? Does our doctrine allow for an outpouring of the Spirit – the "gale" of the Spirit coming upon us individually and collectively? (Lloyd-Jones, *The Puritans*, p. 302)

Still others suffer from the paralysis of low expectations. They go to church and go through the familiar routine of singing, prayer and a sermon, secure in their own salvation and the correctness of their beliefs. Only one thing is missing: the possibility that God might turn up in person and make his presence felt. It simply no longer registers as a real possibility that God might come upon his Church by the Holy Spirit. If ever they allowed for such an experience, they have long since abandoned any expectation that their service might be overtaken by the awesome touch of God's holy fire. This is a desperate paralysis of unbelief, of which the Apostle Paul warned: "There will be terrible times in the last days . . . having a form of godliness but denying its power" (2 Tim 3:1, 5).

As Martyn Lloyd-Jones expressed it:

. . . there is no conception that God may suddenly meet with them, and that something tremendous may happen . . . How often does this vital idea enter into our minds that we are in the presence of the living God, that the Holy Spirit is in the Church, that we may feel the touch of his power? (Lloyd-Jones, *Revival*, p. 72)

Whenever the Church learns to worship the Lord in Spirit as well as in Truth, we break free from such empty and arid formality. Wherever the Spirit is moving in power we quickly learn to expect the unexpected.

Some are stuck, sitting on the fence
They explain that they are waiting for absolute certainty. They want the evidence for this outpouring of the Spirit to be totally watertight before they are prepared to commit

themselves and enter in. "I want to see enough fruit," they explain. "At the moment there's still ambiguity, too much room for doubt." Jonathan Edwards faced the same resistance. Some claimed delay was judicious, since they saw difficulties, or "tares" at present. Edwards considered such an argument spurious:

> If they wait to see a work of God without difficulties and stumbling-blocks, it will be like the fool's waiting by the river side to have the water all run by. A work of God without stumbling-blocks is never to be expected. "It must needs be that offences come." (J Edwards, *Distinguishing Marks*, p. 133)

For others the problem is not the tares but their own indecision. They remain trapped in hesitancy, not prepared to make their mind up and get involved. If someone is genuinely open and undecided, we should expect and encourage them to investigate the evidence thoroughly. One or two encounters cannot satisfy a genuine seeker after truth. They should make every effort to attend meetings and enquire into the experiences of others whose judgment and spiritual maturity they trust. It really will not do for someone to claim that they cannot yet be sure whether this is a work of God and then avoid going to the very meetings where they could see the evidence for themselves. If someone claims an open mind but strenuously avoids all such meetings, their real problem is likely to be not indecision, but fear or prejudice, masquerading as an open mind. This time of refreshing is no secretive or hole in the corner affair, for every week sees an increase in the number of churches influenced. Those who are genuinely prepared to examine the evidence will not find it difficult to be persuaded by the undeniable fruit of a genuine and powerful work of God.

There is always a danger that some will see the blessing pass them by, remaining detached until their opportunity to receive has been lost. Even in the Great Awakening some continued to prevaricate, and Jonathan Edwards urged them to delay no more:

This pretended prudence, in persons waiting so long before they acknowledged this work, will probably in the end prove the greatest imprudence . . . While the glorious fountain is set open in so wonderful a manner, and multitudes flock to it and receive a rich supply for the wants of their souls, they stand at a distance, doubting, wondering, and receiving nothing, and are like to continue thus till the precious season is past. (J Edwards, *Distinguishing Marks,* p. 134)

Anyone whose mind is stubbornly closed by fear or prejudice, despite the witness of the Bible and the history of revivals, will be convinced by no fruit, no matter how great. The solemn warning of history is that those who hesitate too long run the risk of missing out completely on a time of refreshing. They may even miss out on revival itself.

As for all who are prepared to open themselves to God, we rapidly discover that the Lord always has more for every single one of us to receive. If we keep asking for prayer, refusing to be easily deterred if there is slow progress at first, and if we allow the Holy Spirit full freedom to deal with the internal barriers, a spring of life will begin to well up within. Those who open themselves to the living God will in time experience such a flood of divine blessing, they will become amazed that once they found it hard to receive.

Chapter 9

VITAL SIGNS
– OF AN OUTPOURING OF
THE HOLY SPIRIT

In early summer 1994, when the time of refreshing began to register in Britain, a journalist phoned me for an initial assessment. I stressed that the external manifestations, however dramatic, must always be understood to be secondary to meeting with God. Although I felt that the first signs were hopeful that this new wave of the Spirit was neither superficial nor trivial, the acid test was still to be faced: would it lead to an increased number of conversions?

Conversion is by no means the only result of the work of the Holy Spirit, and so my acid test was too narrow. Nevertheless, in any period of true revival an enormous increase in the number of conversions is soon apparent. On the day of Pentecost, when the first Christians were clothed with power just as Jesus had promised, there were no less than 3,000 conversions. As the story of the early church unfolds, Luke shows considerable eagerness to record further milestones of rapid growth as the Spirit continues to be poured out in revival power (Acts 2:47, 4:4, 5:14, 6:7).

The statistics of the major evangelical revivals tell the same story. The Great Awakening followed years in which church leaders complained of a lean harvest: ". . . the gospel has not had any eminent success. Conversions have been rare and dubious; few sons and daughters have been born to God; and the hearts of Christians not so quickened, warmed, and refreshed . . . as they have been" (J Edwards, *Distinguishing Marks*, p. 77). Estimates of the number converted during the revival range from 25,000 and 50,000. This total becomes all the more striking when we realise that the entire population of New England at that time was about 250,000. In other words, the total percentage of population converted at that time was nothing less than ten to twenty per cent. Later revivals saw even larger numbers come to Christ. In 1830 some 100,000 were converted in the United States. Between 1857 and 1859, no less than half a million Americans were born again. This same period saw revivals in several European countries resulting in around 200,000 converts in Sweden, 100,000 in Ulster and 50,000 in Wales. When the Spirit moves in revival power, the harvest becomes so great as to be incomparably beyond the normal effectiveness of the Church.

So how does our present experience compare? While it has been wonderful to experience a "time of refreshing from the presence of the Lord", it is completely unrealistic to speak in terms of revival unless a flood tide of conversions begins. In the final chapter I will address the need to move up through the gears, from refreshing to revival, but first we need to face another major issue. Everyone says that we need to judge an outpouring of the Spirit not merely by the manifestations, but rather by the fruit. So what fruit can we expect? What are the vital signs of an outpouring of the Spirit of God?

From studying the New Testament we can identify no less than thirty-six signs of life, including conversions. This provides a checklist of vital signs that is certainly comprehensive, even though it makes no claim to be exhaustive. I do not wish to imply that all the signs are present with equal force in every outpouring. Nonetheless, they are all biblical indicators. The more these signs increase, the more confident we can be that we are indeed experiencing a significant new wave of the Spirit.

The Spirit glorifies Jesus

Shortly before his death Jesus gave the disciples clear instructions about the coming of the Holy Spirit and explained that the Spirit's delight is to draw attention to the Son. The Spirit's great task is to testify about Christ (John 15:26) and bring him glory (John 16:14). John's first letter provides a test to disclose false spirits and false prophets. Only the Spirit of God will freely acknowledge the truth of the incarnation, that is, that "Jesus Christ has come in the flesh" (1 John 4:1–3). The Holy Spirit has a floodlight ministry, for his first priority is to bring glory to Christ.

The Spirit brings submission to Jesus as Lord

If John's proof of the presence of the Holy Spirit is about truth, Paul's is about faith: "No-one who is speaking by the Spirit of God says, 'Jesus be cursed,' and no one can say, 'Jesus is Lord,' except by the Holy Spirit" (1 Cor 12:3). To be sure, this is a truth statement about the divinity of Christ, for the Greek word, *kurios*, was a word used by Greek-speaking Jews to speak of God himself. But it is also a statement of personal commitment: to confess Christ's Lordship is to accept his mastery. It is the confession of a disciple. Therefore, where the Spirit is being poured out in great measure we can expect a greater willingness not only to confess the truth of Christ's Lordship, but also to embrace the demands of practical discipleship with renewed seriousness.

The Spirit invokes repentance before God's holiness

When Isaiah saw a vision of the manifest presence of the Lord he despaired of life. Before the holiness of God his own uncleanness was unmasked beyond all denial (Isa 6:1–4). Similarly, Jesus explained that the Holy Spirit would convict the world of sin, righteousness and judgment (John 16:8). In previous revivals there has been widespread and overwhelming conviction of sin. Wesley and Whitefield often describe people suffering days of anguish, faced with the recognition of their own sinfulness and the terrible prospect of facing the judgment of God and everlasting damnation. Jonathan Edwards' most famous sermon was entitled "Sinners in the hands of an angry God". One eyewitness, Benjamin Trumbull, described the impact in Enfield, New England as the Holy Spirit empowered the message: "When they went into the meeting-house the appearance of the assembly was thoughtless and vain; the people scarcely conducted themselves with common decency." By the end of the meeting revival had broken out: "Many of the hearers were seen unconsciously holding themselves up against the pillars, and the sides of the pews, as though they already felt themselves sliding into the pit."

In an age of moral relativism, when everyone considers it an absolute right to live according to their own values, it will be a sure and certain sign of the work of the Holy Spirit when many begin to come under real conviction of sin. What is more, there is nothing more deeply unfashionable in the Church than to speak of judgment and hell. Nothing less than the Spirit of God will be able to bring to our decadent society such a life-changing recognition of the seriousness of sin and the urgent need for heartfelt repentance.

The Spirit engenders awe and worship before God's glory
Where the Holy Spirit moves, there is abundant worship. The first impact of the Spirit on the day of Pentecost was a glorious eruption of praise. Because the Spirit also brings a revelation of the glory of God, his presence also brings an overwhelming sense of awe. When John fell as if dead before his vision of Christ he was literally awestruck, totally disarmed by the holy splendour (Rev 1:12–18). Such revelations of the glory of God will lead to high-volume outbursts of joyous praise and also to silence. Not the silence of a court or examination room, but a silence pregnant with the awesome presence of God in his holy majesty.

The Spirit stirs up hunger for God's Word
We would caricature Paul to suggest he is an Apostle of spiritual power alone. Rather he is the Apostle of truth and power, the Apostle of the Word and the Spirit. What he preaches in power is nothing less than the truth of the gospel (1 Thess 1:5). The Spirit does not come in power indiscriminately, but specifically upon those gathered in the name of Jesus (1 Cor 5:4). What is more, the same Holy Spirit breathed the Scriptures into being as the inspired Word of God (2 Tim 3:16). Paul advises Timothy that the servant of God is thoroughly equipped for every good work not simply by being clothed with the power of the Spirit

but by studying the Bible (2 Tim 3:16–17). Although Paul anticipated demonstrations of the Spirit's power, he also commanded Timothy to keep the discipline of preaching the Word (2 Tim 4:2). Above all, the Spirit who comes in power is also the ultimate defender of the truth. Therefore, when Paul urges Timothy to guard the sound teaching of the gospel, he can speak of the invaluable help of the Spirit in this task (2 Tim 1:14). The selfsame integration of Word and Spirit is found in the priorities of the Apostles in Jerusalem, when they resolve to devote themselves both to prayer and to "the ministry of the word" (Acts 6:4).

Some attempt to partition the Word and the Spirit, to set them against one another as alternative or conflicting sources of inspiration and authority, suggesting that it is possible or even necessary to choose between them. Such arguments completely fail to understand the way that the Word and the Spirit are dynamically yoked in the New Testament. Those resources that God has joined together, let no one divide! Without the Spirit's power, we will never know renewal or revival. Without the Word of Truth, we will fail to discern the Spirit and slip imperceptibly into excess and fanaticism. As God breathes afresh upon his Church today it is essential for evangelicals and charismatics alike to learn to live under these twin authorities: the Word, on which we base our convictions, and equally the Spirit, from whom we receive our empowering. Revival is always strengthened by a dynamic yoking of the Word and the Spirit. When the Holy Spirit is poured out upon the Church, he eagerly stirs up renewed hunger for the Word that he inspired.

By the Spirit we receive God's love
The love of God is no mere theoretical proposition. Paul prayed earnestly that believers might know ever more of the infinite splendour of the love of God, not as a concept but in living experience: "And I pray that you, being rooted and established in love, may have power, together with all the saints, to grasp how wide and long and high and deep is the love of Christ, and to know this love that surpasses

knowledge – that you may be filled to the measure of all the fullness of God" (Eph 3:17–19).

Out of his deep love for the disciples Jesus reassured them they would not be left alone: he would ask the Father to send the Spirit as the new instrument of divine love (John 14:16–17). When Paul wrote to the Roman church he described an experience in the past tense which he confidently assumed they fully shared with him: "And hope does not disappoint us, because God has poured his love into our hearts" (Rom 5:5). Paul adds a further phrase in which he recognises the only way by which God's love can penetrate so deep into our inner being – "by the Holy Spirit, whom he has given us" (Rom 5:5). The Spirit of love is the "Spirit of sonship . . . by him we cry, 'Abba, Father'" (Rom 8:15; Gal 4:6). He brings to our spirit a revelation of our new status as God's adopted children, but also of God's immense and tender fatherly love (Rom 8:16). The more we receive the Holy Spirit, the more we know this amazing love.

The Spirit stirs up thirst for God

Isaiah captured a sense of spiritual thirst through the image of streams in the desert (Isa 32:2, 35:6, 43:19–20). Jesus explicitly echoed this picture when he gave his own invitation to receive the Holy Spirit: "If anyone thirsts, let him come to me and drink. Whoever believes in me, as the Scripture has said, streams of living water will flow from within him" (John 7:37–8). Although rainfall is hardly a rarity in England, in the Middle East its arrival is always welcome. When the heavy rains of spring soak into the desert a hidden world bursts into view. The ground is so parched that the rain sinks away in moments, as if none had fallen, but then the desert flowers rise up and bloom. Their time is short, but their appearance is unforgettable. When the Spirit is moving in power he stirs up such a thirst that we discover the desert within. These are the first words on the lips of many Christians seeking prayer in a time of refreshing: "I feel so very dry."

Isaiah also uses the symbol of water in a more horticultural metaphor: "You will be like a well-watered garden" (Isa 58:11). Throughout many centuries it has been the custom in Israel for the gardens of the rich to be cultivated with a lavish use of water. The Garden Tomb in Jerusalem is a modern example of such a garden: always being watered, always full of luxuriant greenery and fragrance. In a sun-scorched land there is a huge contrast between the scrubby trees of the rest of the city and the cool shade and fertile beauty of a well-watered garden. A single shower cannot produce a well-watered garden. In a recent rarity – a hot summer in England – my father-in-law described his method for watering plants: "You can't just tickle them with water. That makes it worse for them. What they need is a good soaking." For the Lord to make us into well-watered gardens the Spirit must stir up a continuing thirst. What we need is not a single shower but a regular drenching in rivers of living water.

The Spirit restores our passion for God

The two most quoted phrases from the letters to the seven churches in the book of Revelation are surely these. To the Ephesians: "Yet I hold this against you: You have forsaken your first love" (Rev 2:4).

And to the Laodiceans: "Because you are lukewarm – neither hot nor cold – I am about to spit you out of my mouth" (Rev 3:16). We often see the Holy Spirit tackling both problems. When the fire of living faith has burnt low, whether through distraction, exhaustion or disappointment, he draws us back to a heart relationship with Father God. As a result we hear frequent testimonies about falling in love with Jesus all over again. Similarly, when our commitment has become feeble and compromised, he rekindles our passion for obedience and active discipleship.

The Spirit presses upon us the presence of God

We saw in Chapter Two that while God is omnipresent, there is also a manifest presence of God, so arresting that it is more real and immediate than anything we can see, hear or touch with our physical senses. This is not something automatic or universal, nor a fancy way of describing normal Christian experience. When the Spirit is poured out in power, believers and unbelievers alike begin to cry out: "He is here, he is here!

Surely God is in this place!" Sarah Edwards' experiences, referred to in Chapter Three, are a glowing example of the amazing intensity of experiences of God's presence. At such times the Christian is captivated as never before by the wonder and love of the living God: "His nearness to me and my dearness to him".

The Spirit releases God's power

God's power is like his love and his presence: not an intellectual concept but a dynamic reality. For Paul, the effectiveness of his preaching was not produced by wise and persuasive words, but "with a demonstration of the Spirit's power" (1 Cor 2:4). He wanted churches to be filled with people whose faith did not rest on their minister's learning or eloquence, personality or pastoral gifts, but upon God's power (1 Cor 2:5). God's Kingdom, he explained, is not about words and talk but about power from on high (1 Cor 4:20). Paul expects local churches to experience manifestations of this power both when they meet together (1 Cor 5:4), and in their individual lives (1 Cor 6:19). This all surpassing power comes only from God (2 Cor 4:7), for nothing less than the power which raised Jesus from the dead is now at work within us (Eph 1:19, 3:20). Paul urges the Ephesians to be strong in the Lord "and in his mighty power" (Eph 6:10) and reminds Timothy that the Spirit given by God is the "spirit of power" (2 Tim 1:7). When the Spirit of God is poured out upon the Church we discover anew God's power and see an overflow of his mighty works.

The Spirit provides assurance of salvation

To be confident of salvation is the birthright of every believer, and we can draw on three key resources, the Bible, our lives and the inner witness of the Spirit. The Bible is the Spirit's great gift to the Church: as we study the Scriptures we lay hold of the written promises that guarantee our salvation by faith in Christ. No matter how we feel, no matter how we let God down, the promises of Scripture remain a rock-solid foundation.

Our lives bear witness to the Spirit's active presence.

Changes in our character demonstrate that we really have been born again. No matter how flawed our lives remain, where we discover a new delight in God's law, the emergence of new holiness and love, we trace the handiwork of the Spirit who has come to live within.

Paul taught clearly a third source of assurance: "The Spirit himself testifies with our spirit that we are God's children" (Rom 8:16). This inner testimony is the highest kind of assurance. Neither derived from the Scriptures nor deduced from our lives, it is the direct gift of the Holy Spirit to the inner being of the believer. Tragically, much Bible-believing Christianity has become so paranoid about the dangers of trusting in feelings, that this highest form of assurance has often been veiled in neglect or even actively discouraged, as subjective, non-rational and unreliable. The cries of joy among the crowds listening to John Wesley and George Whitefield were derived neither from scriptural promises nor changes in character, even though both continue to be invaluable means of assurance. When the Spirit flows in revival power he gives confidence of salvation by his direct, inward testimony, and our hearts begin to fill with joy. As we saw in Chapter Five, only where the Spirit of God is flooding our lives can we expect to experience what Peter calls "an inexpressible and glorious joy" (1 Pet 1:8).

The Spirit strengthens our confidence in the gospel
Many Christians in our society feel almost obliged to apologise for personal faith and going to church. Some unbelievers patronise and scorn us, treating our convictions as antiquated and eccentric, surplus to requirements in the modern world. Others condemn us out of hand as narrow-minded, stupid or naive. This can make believers defensive or even apologetic, reluctant to own up to their faith and wary about witnessing. But when the Spirit is poured out upon us, he lights up anew the great doctrines of the faith, renewing our confidence not merely in God's existence, but in his power to save. Think of Peter, preaching the gospel before the Sanhedrin, who had hauled him before their court to suppress his preaching: "It is by the name of Jesus Christ of Nazareth, whom you crucified

but whom God raised from the dead, that this man stands before you healed" (Acts 4:10). Luke underlines the source of these unyielding convictions by stressing that Peter was "filled with the Holy Spirit" (Acts 4:8). Confidence in the gospel is a hallmark of the Spirit's reviving presence.

The Spirit brings a passion for the lost

Where there is renewed confidence in the gospel there is also a new depth of concern for evangelism. When the church in Jerusalem was faced with persecution they didn't simply pray for protection and then keep their heads down. Rather, they prayed: "Now, Lord, consider their threats and enable your servants to speak your word with great boldness" (Acts 4:29). Luke records that the results of their prayer were that the room was shaken, all were filled afresh with the Holy Spirit, and they spoke out boldly (Acts 4:31). In the present refreshing we have seen some discover a new zeal in ardent prayer for the lost, sometimes with weeping and fasting. Others are finding and seizing more opportunities for personal witness than ever before. For refreshing to turn into revival this burden for the lost will need to intensify and spread.

The Spirit brings compassion for the poor

At the launch of his public ministry Jesus quoted from Isaiah 61: "The Spirit of the Lord is on me, because he has anointed me to preach good news to the poor" (Luke 4:18). It is quite impossible to read the Old Testament prophets without recognising that the Spirit of God is passionate about justice. Our God is the defender of the poor. For some Western Christians the period of the Cold War produced a reluctance to accept this scriptural priority. A familiar objection could be heard: "Isn't that just communism with a religious face?" Our Christian mandate is much older than Marx. A fine example of the Spirit bringing compassion for the poor is found in George Whitefield. The most powerful of the revival preachers, passionate for the salvation of the lost, on his arrival in the States one of his first actions was to establish an orphanage for the children of settlers. The same

Spirit brings a burden of compassion for both immediate and eternal needs.

The Spirit propels an increase in world mission

The Spirit who brings a burden for the lost cannot leave Christians with narrow horizons. The mission task is global, for God so loved the entire world that he gave his only Son. When the church at Antioch had put together a five-star leadership team, the Holy Spirit spoke and asked for Saul and Barnabas to be released for world mission (Acts 13:2). Where the Spirit is moving in power Christians take up the mantle of world mission. Small wonder that Britain has been without revival for so long, when for around a century the total number of British missionaries has been in steady decline. A church that claims to be open to the Spirit but has no interest in world mission knows little of the Spirit of God.

The Spirit promotes intercessory prayer

Both the Son and the Spirit intercede for us, but the Spirit also has the task of helping us to pray (Rom 8:26, 27, 34). Where the Spirit is being poured out upon the Church, we can expect an upsurge in attendance at prayer meetings, increased discipline in making time to pray and a greater boldness and fervency in prayer. Prayer meetings cease to be the Cinderella of the Church and become again the engine room of sustained advance which we see in Acts 4.

The Spirit generates empowered preaching

Paul described his own preaching as gospel truth proclaimed "with power, with the Holy Spirit and with deep conviction" (1 Thess 1:5). The Great Awakening saw a recovery of such vibrant proclamation, following a period in which sermons had degenerated into lifeless lectures. There must be sound doctrine and thorough preparation – witty stories are not enough. But addresses that merely stimulate the cerebral cortex are not worthy of the name of preaching. As Martyn Lloyd-Jones insisted: "There must be warmth and heat as well as light" (Lloyd-Jones, *The Puritans*, p. 368). There is nothing as powerful as anointed preaching to open the living truths of the gospel to Christian and non-believer alike. Every lasting revival has known a re-invigoration of this God-appointed form of communication: preaching empowered by the Holy Spirit's fire.

The Spirit enlarges love of truth

Jesus described the Holy Spirit as the Spirit of truth (John 16:13). Whenever the Spirit comes in power there is not only a hunger for the Bible, which we considered earlier, there is also a deeper love of truth and a new eagerness to learn more. The study of the Bible, doctrine and Christian history all become more urgent and attractive tasks. The sales and standards of Christian books will increase when the Spirit of truth is moving freely, as will enrolment in Christian study courses.

The Spirit increases spiritual fruit

Some might have expected this entire chapter to be devoted to the fruit of the Spirit (Gal 5:22–3). To do so would have meant neglecting many other vital signs, some of which have become less familiar. To be sure, these noble qualities are indisputable indicators of the Spirit's work. Together they describe the character of Christ towards which the Spirit continues to transform us (2 Cor 3:18). Although there are moments of crisis in the Christian life which result in sudden spurts of advance in holiness, on the whole the spiritual fruit grows steadily. Christian character is the produce of a lifetime. Nonetheless, we can expect a time of refreshing or revival to become a hothouse for the fruit of the Spirit, leading to some measure of rapid and undeniable progress in holiness.

The Spirit promotes growth in humility

The first taste of spiritual power often leads to temptations of pride. But the more we know of the Spirit of God the more we discover our own need for humility. Paul describes the amazing treasure of the Holy Spirit within the believer, but he also speaks freely of himself, in his sinfulness and frailty, as an earthen vessel. Paul is not suffering from low self-esteem. Rather he has clearly grasped God's strategy: the reason for the contrast between our own inadequacy and the glorious treasure of the Holy Spirit is "to show that this all-surpassing power is from God and not from us" (2 Cor 4:7). The Christian who boasts in his own strength and accomplishments knows little of the Holy Spirit. He humbles as he fills.

The Spirit inflames generous giving

The finest evidence for this important sign is Paul's description of the Macedonian church (2 Cor 8:1–5). He describes the condition of this church in three phrases, two of which hardly point to a prospect of substantial giving, for they are suffering a "most severe trial" and live in "extreme poverty". However, a third quality cuts right across their blighted circumstances, for in the Holy Spirit they are experiencing "overflowing joy". Not only does the joy overflow, presumably in exuberant praise, they also experience a welling up of "rich generosity", giving so generously that Paul is almost embarrassed, for they give even beyond their means. This is supernatural giving, which goes against the grain of normal money management. When the Spirit flows into our lives, the cash flows out.

The Spirit increases love for one another

The love command is at the heart of Jesus's teaching (John 13:34–5). Therefore, the more the Spirit brings us the love of the Father and the Son, the more we can expect our love for one another to grow. In the time of refreshing I have seen relationships mended, as those who receive powerfully from God then pick up the phone, write a letter or see someone face to face, to say sorry or offer forgiveness. The Spirit prompts us to make the first move. Old scores are no longer settled, they are torn up and forgotten. This increase of love wells up not only within the Church, but at least as much within marriages and families. No professional counsellor can work as powerfully and deeply as our loving God. When the Holy Spirit comes in power upon a marriage he ignites new fires of love and intimacy.

The Spirit's outpouring leads to opposition and persecution
It may seem paradoxical or even contradictory to turn to increased opposition, immediately after considering increased love. But this is the unchanging pattern of Christian history. Though the first Christians in Jerusalem were united in love, they became reviled by their fellow Jews as divisive in their convictions and behaviour. In order to promote the unity of the Church in faithful obedience to the gospel, Paul had to become tireless in condemning and excluding the false teachers, who inevitably denounced him in turn. What was true of the first generation has always remained true. We saw in Chapter Three just how intense and aggressive the opposition can become in times of revival.

Regrettably, when the Spirit comes in power, opposition is not far behind. It comes not only from those outside the Church, but also from some professing Christians: both establishment churchmen who find such enthusiasm deeply distasteful and also some hidebound evangelicals, blinded by their own rigidity, unable to recognise or receive the Spirit of Christ when he comes in power.

The Spirit exposes unclean spirits
The Holy Spirit and unclean spirits are like matter and anti-matter: they don't mix. In Jesus's ministry we see that where the life of God breaks out upon the face of the earth there is a tremendous surge of spiritual opposition. Demons could not conceal their presence when the Son of God came to town (for example in Luke 4:33–4, 41; 8:26–33). The same pattern is repeated in Acts. When the followers of Jesus are empowered by the Holy Spirit, they face an onslaught of unmasked demons (for example, Acts 5:16, 8:7, 16:16–18). When the Spirit is poured out in revival power the light of Christ burns bright. We therefore must expect that any church enjoying an increase of the Holy Spirit will also see a greater measure of demonic manifestation. This is nothing

to be frightened about, for Jesus has already won the victory
(Col 2:15).

The Spirit pours out spiritual gifts

In the book of Acts, wherever the Holy Spirit comes in power
there is a fresh eruption of spiritual gifts. The greater the
outpouring, the greater the release of spiritual gifts that we
can expect. Existing gifts will be enlarged, new gifts will be
received. In the present day, the widespread restoration of
spiritual gifts points to the Holy Spirit preparing the Church
for a mighty advance.

The Spirit provides healings, signs and wonders

Luke describes Jesus's healing ministry in terms that may
seem surprising: "And the power of the Lord was present
for him to heal the sick" (Luke 5:17). It seems that even the
incarnate Son of God needed to know the manifest presence
of God's power for healings to happen. Small wonder that
the first Christians prayed for spiritual power: "Stretch out
your hand to heal and perform miraculous signs and wonders
through the name of your holy servant Jesus" (Acts 4:30).
The direct result of their prayer was that the Holy Spirit came
upon them in power once more (Acts 4:31). If we want to
know healings, signs and wonders, we need earnestly to seek
the power of the Holy Spirit.

The Spirit increases faith and expectancy

This proposition is hardly surprising, given some of the other
vital signs we have explored. But for many people, church is
the last place to look for any excitement or drama. All we
expect is the same boring old routine, as it was in the beginning, as dull as for ever. Not so the early church: "Everyone
was filled with awe, and many wonders and miraculous signs
were done by the apostles" (Acts 2:43). When a church is in
revival, people travel to services filled with expectancy. In the
meeting they are on the edge of their seats, wondering what
God is going to do next. We expect more, ask for more, see
more and receive more. Instead of being satisfied with going

through the motions, our churches become again the dwelling place of God, in majesty and awesome power.

The Spirit creates a longing for heaven

We saw in Chapter Two that the Holy Spirit is described in the New Testament as the firstfruit, the seal of ownership, the downpayment or deposit (Rom 8:23; 2 Cor 1:22; Eph 1:13). The more the Spirit is poured out upon the Church, the more he brings the presence of the future, days of heaven on earth. This traffic is two-way, for as we take delight in a foretaste of heaven, we grow more eager for the fulfilment of heaven itself. Paul spoke frankly about this longing for heaven: "I desire to depart and be with Christ, which is better by far" (Phil 1:23). In times of revival, as heaven becomes more immediate in our experience, the Christian appetite increases for resurrection life.

The Spirit stirs up expectations of the second coming

When the Spirit brings days of heaven to earth, Christians naturally begin to wonder whether the end is at hand. In every revival the second coming of Christ returns to centre-stage. Christians become more eager and expectant, examining the signs of the times. It cannot be proven, of course, but the conviction gradually gathers pace that this could indeed be the final great period of harvest before the return of the King of kings.

The Spirit releases new creativity

The Holy Spirit is dynamic and creative, intimately involved in the artistry of the natural world. In times of refreshing and revival we can expect his creativity to rub off upon believers. At such times there has always been a tremendous outburst of worship, new songs expressing the vitality of a faith that is vibrant with life, bubbling with joy and burning with passion for God. The vast and enduring output of Charles Wesley and Isaac Watts speaks for itself. We can also confidently predict the emergence of new preachers, new writers, new magazines, new bands, new Christian organisations, and in our day new uses of multimedia communications. When the Spirit comes in power, a ferment of creativity is sure to be released.

The Spirit inspires new ways of being church

This same creativity will also lead to the re-invention of the Church. One major spur to this creativity is the urgency of cultural engagement, which is always a priority for the Spirit. As I explored in another book, *21st Century Church*, the Holy Spirit is the spirit of mission, always passionate about bridging the gap to those who feel alienated from traditional church culture – the style, language, buildings, etc. When Paul planted churches in the gentile world he was creating new ways of being church, rather than just duplicating the pattern of the original Jewish churches. For the sake of the gospel he abandoned his own traditions. Something as simple as open-air preaching was unthinkable to many in England, including John Wesley, before the time of the Great Awakening. For the sake of the lost, Wesley and Whitefield stood against the church prejudice that decried such methods as unseemly and irreverent. When Hudson Taylor "went native" as a missionary in China, he put the need of the Chinese to hear the gospel in a way they could understand and receive above the preferences of his own cultural background. As the Spirit is poured out upon our generation, such creativity is sure to spring up anew within the Church.

A second major springboard for creativity and experiment comes not from seeking to make an impact upon the lost but as a result of the impact the Holy Spirit has upon us. Some churches will find themselves bewildered by the sudden surge of spiritual vitality. They may simply not know how to cope, with the result that the new outpouring of the Spirit finds no outlet in their activities and services. They may try to ignore it, in the hope that it will go away. They may try to suppress it, because it rocks the boat of familiar Christianity. In short, some old wineskins will be put under considerable strain. The new wine will create a ferment of experiment. New wineskins, new ways of being church, will prove both inevitable and vital.

The Spirit encourages non-denominational co-operation
One of the charges against George Whitefield was that he engaged in "un-Anglican activities". He not only suggested that some leaders in his own church had little grasp of the gospel of salvation, he also had the temerity to preach in buildings owned by Presbyterians and Baptists. This is always the pattern of periods of revival. When evangelicalism is on fire with the Spirit of God, our common faith in Christ takes priority over any denominational allegiance. Denominations pale into insignificance beside the glorious task of taking good news to a lost world. I think it was D L Moody who once declared that if he had found a drop of denominationalism in his blood, he would gladly slit his veins.

I am not suggesting for one moment that anyone need despise their denomination or stream. We simply need to keep them in their place. In the history of revivals, no revival has ever begun through the organised activities or official channels of a denomination. No revival has ever stayed narrowly within a single denomination. Indeed, denominational leaders are often outspoken opponents of revival or the last to come on board. When the Spirit of God is in revival flood, he breaks the banks of restrictive human structures and organisations, catching us up together in a mighty torrent of the life of heaven.

The Spirit increases the number of candidates for full-time ministry
When the Spirit moves in power, the gospel is seen in all its splendour and evangelistic urgency is reborn. In such a climate, we see our lives, careers and destinies from the perspective of eternity. As a result, the numbers and calibre of those prepared to give up everything for the sake of the gospel are sure to increase. A powerful move of the Spirit fills up the Bible colleges and creates queues at the doors of missionary societies. Not just for short-term service for a year or two, but for a lifetime of service and sacrifice for Jesus Christ and his world.

The Spirit brings freedom to captives

Everyone who comes to faith in Christ is given a double liberation. We are set free from the dominion of darkness (Col 1:13) and given freedom to approach God with new confidence (Eph 3:12). Through the death of Christ our liberation is secure. In him we are free indeed (John 8:36; Gal 5:1).

Christians are born again into freedom, but everywhere are found in chains. There are chains of legalism and judgmentalism. These are usually imposed with the best of intentions, namely to obey the New Testament warnings not to abuse our new freedom for sensual indulgence (Gal 5:13; 1 Pet 2:16). What results is a return to the religion of the Pharisees, a shadow-world that is narrow, negative and constantly fault-finding. There are chains of anxiety, where the mind is captive within a swamp of worries; if one problem is solved, two more emerge to take its place. There are chains of destructive relationships and habits, which promise fulfilment and happiness but exact the price of psychological captivity and addiction. There are chains of bitterness where a grievance is nursed for years. There are chains of work. While some wonder whether they will ever work again, others are prisoners to their career which demands to be their top priority and consumes every waking hour.

Paul explained the revolution that the Holy Spirit can bring: "Where the Spirit of the Lord is, there is freedom" (2 Cor 3:17). When the Spirit comes in power, our eternal status has a revolutionary impact upon our daily living. The freedom of heaven comes down to earth. The Spirit of liberation lightens our burdens and puts a fresh spring in our step. We receive a new experience of liberation, a new opportunity to break free from our chains with the help of the living God. Freedom is no longer something just to look forward to, it becomes a way of life.

The Spirit releases abundant life

Jesus promised he had come to bring life in all its abundance (John 10:10). Therefore, when the flow of the Spirit is running high, we can expect Christians to come alive as never before.

Life takes on an extra dimension in our relationships, our work and leisure, and above all in our walk with God. Our whole approach to life will be marked by a new joie de vivre, a new passion for Christ.

Abundant life is both a vital sign in itself and it encapsulates all the other vital signs. The prodigal son scoured the world in search of great parties, but when he finally came home to his father's house, he discovered the best party of all. When God pours out the Spirit, it is party time in the Church. A party of love and holiness, of liberation and joy. The time has come for days of heaven on earth.

Chapter 10

MORE LORD!
– FROM REFRESHING TO REVIVAL

One summer we visited La Torche, one of the best surfing beaches in France. At regular intervals along the beach are stark warning signs, explaining that swimming is strictly prohibited. The waves are too powerful, the hidden currents deceptively strong. A hundred yards from shore many surfers were bobbing on the sea, crouched on their boards, waiting intently to ride upon only the biggest and most powerful waves. On a cold and windswept afternoon, no one else was in the water, not even paddling, let alone attempting to swim. Suddenly one young man could no longer resist displaying his strength. Ignoring all the warning signs, spurred on by the desire to impress his girl-friend, he stripped to his trunks and threw himself into the sea. It was not difficult to recognise an experienced and strong swimmer in his easy, powerful stroke.

Swimming out from the shore he seemed to make mockery of the warning signs. As he turned to swim back his arms continued to stretch out, confident and strong, but in an instant his rate of advance fell to nothing. Beating against the sea with every stroke, mighty waves crashing over him as they raced towards the beach, he made no forward movement at all. The greatest efforts of a powerful swimmer were neutralised by the undertow. As he grew exhausted he trod water, changed stroke, struggled to stay calm and survive. Eventually he shaped himself to be as much of an obstruction to every wave as possible; they began to throw him towards land, even though when each wave passed by, he was sucked again towards the open sea. Stumbling at last on to the sand he had lost all trace of bravado and swagger. A lucky man, he had narrowly escaped with his life after swimming against the undertow.

Days of crisis

The Church in the western world has had a similar experience in the twentieth century, swimming against the undertow of a society that has tried to live without reference to God, often treating Christian faith as little more than superstition or a Sunday morning pastime for a strange religious minority. Atheism and materialism have made unbridled advance. Church attendances have crashed from the heights of the mid-nineteenth century. In recent years, the Church in England has been losing around a thousand people every week, and not all of those have died! Despite our best efforts, many people have treated the Christian faith as surplus to requirements, something left over from a more primitive age. Nonetheless, as the end of the century approaches, many are beginning to take stock of our society and wonder whether, in turning away from Christian faith and morality, civilisation now finds itself having to swim against the undertow. Many are wondering, with increasing anxiety and dread, what kind of world our children's children will inherit.

The drugs menace continues to escalate, so that Douglas Hurd, British Foreign Secretary, has warned that the spectre of illegal drugs is haunting Europe. Official figures suggest there are five million hard drug users within the European Community, including one million addicts. Marijuana use may be as high as twenty to thirty million. One third of all prisoners in Western European jails are there for drug offences. In Newcastle, one recent survey found that eighty per cent of teenagers had sampled either hard or soft drugs. LSD has made a comeback in the nineties, its low street price causing young people to ignore the side-effects which led to its demise at the end of the sixties. Ecstasy, crack cocaine and new designer drugs have all added to this wretched plague, where an evening's entertainment can exact the price of a life. Tony White, head of the British Criminal Intelligence Service, has declared that, following the government's "war on drugs" in recent years, "Law enforcement is getting better and better, but the problem gets worse and worse."

Violent crime has become ever more a way of life. In London, police warn that an explosion in the number of handguns is bringing an American way of death to British streets. In the States, homicide is as American as mom's apple pie, with 24,500 killed in 1993. Young men aged eighteen to twenty-four, the most likely generation to be murdered, are twice as likely to commit murder now compared with ten years ago. Those aged fourteen to seventeen have seen their rate of killing jump by 161 per cent. Young men aged fourteen to seventeen now commit more than half the nation's murders, in a trend that is steadily increasing. Guns and knives are easily available, many videos glorify violence, and young men seem increasingly unrestrained either by moral convictions or fear of being caught and punished. Killing is easy and life is cheap.

In the summer of '94, German police uncovered a black market in nuclear-grade plutonium, making five seizures in five weeks. The Soviet Union's vast stockpile of nuclear weapons is beginning to be dispersed through a new global trade. Hiroaki Takizawa, chief of Interpol's economic crime group, has been forced to acknowledge, "We may now have to start thinking in terms of bombs." The mayor of Palermo, Leoluca Orlando, has alerted the European Parliament that the Sicilian Mafia has begun a lucrative black market in pluto- nium, uranium and arms smuggled from the old Soviet bloc. In urging a rapid response from Europol, the European police agency, he warned, "It's a new gold rush for the Cosa Nostra, a new business with immense possible earnings." After brief years of euphoria at the end of the Soviet-American arms race, it begins to look as if it may be only a matter of time before terrorists, criminal gangs, and unstable dictatorships such as Iraq and Libya begin to shop around for their own nuclear arsenals. A mushroom-shaped cloud still threatens to shroud the future of the planet.

Other crises confronting our society are equally stark. Within the western world and even more severely within the world economy, the crisis of poverty grows worse. The scenario of the Brandt Report, which argued that future world conflict would move from an East-West to a North-South axis, with the developing nations seeking to seize a better deal by force of arms, looks ever more convincing. In personal relationships, everyone is looking for love, but many have forgotten how to keep love alive, for marriage is an ever more fragile union. Teachers across the western world have become counsellors to a generation in pain. Some classes report that well over half the children are living with the heartache of a broken home. The spectre of AIDS continues to gather millions under its curse. Recent figures indicate AIDS is breaking out in Asian countries which previously ignored HIV testing and protection, while in the western world the long expected escalation of the disease in the heterosexual community is now gaining inexorable momentum. Meanwhile in the animal world, rivers continue to die from industrial pollution; the fish stocks of the oceans are facing terminal depletion through a policy of relentless over-fishing; many animal breeds are at the brink of extinction; and the countryside is ravaged by road-building as ever more tarmac scars the land. Alvin Toffler wrote of "future shock", describing our struggle to keep up with changes in the way we live. As the year 2000 draws near, many today are beginning to experience something more than pre-millennial tension. In a society that seems to be running ever more out of control, we discover the experience of "future dread". The brave new world of the twenty-first century looks grim indeed.

Days of opportunity

How can the Church in the western world cultivate genuine hope at the end of the twentieth century? Times of refreshing are wonderful, but they are not enough. We need to see God move us on from refreshing to full-blooded revival. While the reckless swimmer at La Torche was struggling to stay afloat, sucked backwards by the undertow, the surfers continued their sport without struggle or fear. Beneath the surface of the water, the swimmer's body was prey to swirling and perilous currents. On top of their boards, the surfers were immune to the undertow, rising above the currents as they rode the waves. When we struggle in our own strength against the destructive currents of our society, we know what it is to swim against the undertow. When God brings revival to his Church, despite the inevitable backlash of verbal and even physical opposition, we ride the waves of the incoming tide of the Spirit of God. What steps can we take to prepare for the decisive advance of revival?

Our God has not changed

The living God still retains his ancient power to save. Indeed, the rate of conversion growth around the world is accelerating today, with the Church in much of the developing world experiencing faster growth than ever before in Christian history. In Africa, there were estimated in 1945 to be twenty million Christians. By 1978, over thirty years later, this had jumped to seventy million. By 1988, just one decade later, this figure had leaped to a remarkable 250 million. How much in the West today we need African, Asian and South American missionaries, with their intensity of prayer, zeal in service, and great expectancy for God to move in power.

Look back in hope

When Gideon was commanded by the Lord to bring new liberation to Israel, he recalled the power with which God had worked in the time of Moses: "Where are all the wonders that our fathers told us about?" (Judg 6:13). This is not a counsel of despair, but a heartfelt cry for God to stretch out his hand in power once again. When John Wesley looked back on the effectiveness of his many years of ministry as his life drew towards its end, he recognised the astonishing miracle of the divine turnaround. Before God poured out his Spirit in revival, the world was in a wretched condition, addicted to immorality and indifferent to God, while the Church was spiritually inert, morally compromised, and had lost confidence in the Gospel of Christ. What God has done before, he is more than capable of doing again in our generation.

Seize the initiative

When Nehemiah heard about the desolation of Jerusalem, its walls and buildings broken down and blackened with fire, he sat down and wept. In his wretched sadness he turned to God. Fasting and praying he pleaded for mercy for his people. As a result, Nehemiah received more than faith and confidence, for he came to know God's manifest presence, just as in a previous critical period in Israel's history, Moses had "the gracious hand of my God upon me" (Neh 2:18). With God's help, Nehemiah confronted the enormity of the disaster squarely, with no shallow optimism or easy answers, but at the same time he seized the initiative for the glory of God: "You see the trouble we are in: Jerusalem lies in ruins and its gates have been burned with fire. Come, let us rebuild the wall of Jerusalem, and we will no longer be in disgrace" (Neh 2:17). The days of crisis became a day of opportunity.

Recognise our opportunity

Growing and gnawing anxiety about the future of our society could be turned to good purpose by the Church. The death of communism has exposed the limitations of capitalism, for our economic system has consistently proved unable to provide either work or a fair deal for all. The unemployed, the sick and the elderly often struggle. There is a rising tide of disillusionment, not only with political solutions to the great needs of our day, but also with politicians themselves. Political corruption and hypocrisy are seen to be endemic worldwide. We are also experiencing the bankruptcy of materialism which, despite the endless promises of advertising, cannot satisfy our deepest needs. A new dissatisfaction with modern society, a new questing after spiritual realities, a new search for purpose are all emerging as the end of the century approaches. Here is a society which is becoming ever more prepared to hear again the good news of Jesus Christ.

At the same time, we can trace a growing potential

throughout the history of the Protestant Church. During the Reformation, there was a reclamation of the power of the cross, the authority of the Bible, and the glorious doctrine of justification by faith. Through the Great Awakening there was a recovery of the importance of active evangelism, preaching on fire, and the absolute necessity not merely of doctrinal orthodoxy but of personal saving faith. There followed the recovery of another Apostolic priority with the worldwide missionary movement, and then the emergence of the evangelical social conscience, with the result that evangelicals took a lead in campaigning against slavery and championing many major social reforms. In the twentieth century, the Pentecostal and charismatic movements recovered the biblical emphasis on the vital importance of the Holy Spirit. We have also seen a new release of the spiritual gifts known in the early church, together with a recovery of the biblical principle of every member ministry.

For all the failings and weaknesses of the modern Church, we stand at the climax of centuries which have seen, step by step, the restoration of the priorities and practices of the Apostolic era. The Spirit of God has surely been bringing a continuing reformation to the Church, in order to equip us for an advance unparalleled since the first Christian generation. What is more, the globalisation of modern culture and the speed of modern travel and communication together provide the opportunity for revival not merely on a national, but on a global scale. We could be on the brink of the greatest revival in the history of the Church, the revival that precedes the return of Christ. The Bride is being prepared for glory. We have received the Apostolic priorities and practices. Now once again we need to receive the power.

In our weakness, strength
The Holy Spirit is given not as a reward for our success, but so that we can accomplish things for God far beyond our own resources. As Paul taught, the Spirit helps us in our weakness (Rom 8:26). If we acknowledge our weakness as individuals, we are on the road to personal renewal. If we acknowledge the weakness of the western Church, for all our conferences

and expertise, our resources and learning, we are in a position to seek the strength of God. He gives power to the weak, and lifts up those who have learnt to humble themselves before him (1 Pet 5:6).

In our thirst, living water
Jesus's invitation to receive the Holy Spirit was given to all those who are thirsty (John 7:37–9). Spiritual complacency is the mortal enemy of revival. Only when we declare our thirst, and seek ever more from the abundance of God, can we expect to be radically transformed with the life of heaven. Isaiah recorded God's desire to make us a well-watered garden (Isa 58:11). We cannot become such a garden through receiving from God just once or twice. The more the streams flow, the more God can use us. When the Spirit is filling us, his presence overflows from within us to touch the lives of family and neighbours, workmates and friends. Those who cultivate a healthy thirst for the things of God will come to seek not just a few drops but a mighty and continuing downpour of rain from heaven.

In refreshing, stay God-centred
The outpouring of the Spirit is not for the sake of filling our churches; still less is it about seeking glory for ourselves. Nor must we become centred on the manifestations, neither during a refreshing nor during a revival, when the power of the presence of God is multiplied, and manifestations are likely to increase. We must seek God, and God alone. If we become distracted from God, the outpouring will dry up. The fires of heavenly life will burn low among us once again.

For revival, power from on high
When Jesus commanded the disciples to stay in Jerusalem, he taught them the secret of effective service: to be clothed with power from on high (Luke 24:49). The result of their obedience was a church advancing in revival power. There will be no revival for the church that does not earnestly pray for power from on high. Nothing less than a mighty outpouring of the Holy Spirit upon the Church can turn

our society around. Only when the Church is empowered and revived, will the nations be awakened, in repentance and saving faith in Christ.

Through prayer, heaven will be opened
The most important thing to recognise about both refreshings and revival is that this is a work of God. To be sure, we need to prepare ourselves, through repentance and renewed submission to the Lordship of Christ. Above all, we need to learn again to persist in prayer for revival in our generation. During the time of refreshing we have learnt to take time to seek God. The queues for the Eiffel Tower or *The Maid of the Mist* demonstrate that some experiences in life are worth waiting for. How much more do we need to learn to persist in prayer, not only for times of refreshing, wonderful as they are, but for the even mightier outpouring needed to bring revival in our day.

Isaiah provides us with an outstanding example of a prayer for God to move in power, in which he recognises that all he can do is pray, for God alone has the authority to release his power upon the face of the earth.

> Oh, that you would rend the heavens and come down,
> that the mountains would tremble before you!
> As when fire sets twigs ablaze
> and causes water to boil,
> come down to make your name known to your enemies
> and cause the nations to quake before you!
> For when you did awesome things that we did not expect,
> you came down, and the mountains trembled before you.
>   (Isa 64:1–3)

There is nothing that prepares the way for revival so much as earnest prayer. But prayer that has degenerated into an empty ritual is worthless. Finney described a church where they habitually prayed for revival, without the remotest expectation that God would ever do anything among them. Prayer without faith is powerless. Other churches may pray for revival, but reject it when it comes, horrified by the power

of God, by the emotions and manifestations, or by the kind of
people who suddenly start to invade their respectable church.
As Isaiah declares, when God works in power the one thing
we can guarantee is that we will see things we never
expected.

In openness, go deeper into God

Ezekiel's vision of the river of life is a picture that prophesies
the coming of the Holy Spirit (Ezek 47). Starting from
Jerusalem, wherever the river flows it brings life, just as
began to happen when the early church received power
and then moved out from Israel in mission to the world.
The prophecy still applies in the Christian era, as the river
of life continues to flow in the task of local and world mission.
Above all, Ezekiel's vision describes the outpouring of the
Holy Spirit in revival. At first, the water is ankle-deep. A
thousand cubits later it is knee-deep. Another thousand and
it is waist-deep. Still another thousand and it is too deep for
anyone to cross. If we seriously want God to move in revival
power, we have to be prepared to be out of our depth. Duncan
Campbell, who experienced revival on the Isle of Lewis in
1949, used a graphic phrase to capture what is different
about a church in revival: individuals and churches become
"saturated with God". If we are satisfied with anything less,
we will not hunger and thirst for revival. Only if God saturates
our churches with his life and love will holy power break out
upon the land.

In revival, glory in the Church

The glory of God is at the heart of revival. When Paul
prayed for the Ephesians, he did not merely pray that they
would live for the glory of God. His prayer is more startling
and radical: that God's glory might be in the Church (Eph
3:20–1). In revival, God comes down among his people. His
manifest presence overwhelms believers with the splendour
of his holiness, majesty and might. Torrents of divine love
are poured into our hearts, causing an abundant overflow
of joy. As the Church is ignited with the life of Christ,
unbelievers cannot keep away. Though some mock, others

are compelled to come and see for themselves. Revival is more than seeker-sensitive, it is seeker-seizing. In revival, more than at any other time, we see God's glory in the Church.

Nothing is needed more by the world and the Church at the end of the twentieth century than this: a mighty outpouring of the Spirit of God in revival power. Nothing less should burn at the heart of our prayers. As individuals, in local churches and across the land, this needs to be our cry: more Lord! We praise God for the times of refreshing we have been enjoying, but our plea must be that they are no more than a prelude. We long to see the glory and power of the living God sweeping across the face of the earth as never before. A global revival to prepare the world for the return of Christ. Send revival, Lord, and send it in our day!

SELECTED BIBLIOGRAPHY

R Allen, *Missionary Methods – St Paul's or Ours?* Eerdmans, 1991 (first published 1912)

D Bebbington, *Evangelicalism in Modern Britain*, Unwin & Hyman, 1989

C Boyd, *The Apostle of Hope*, Sovereign, 1991

D A Carson, *A Call for Spiritual Reformation*, IVP, 1992

P Y Cho, *Prayer: key to revival*, Word, 1984

A Dallimore, *Spurgeon*, Banner, 1984

A Dallimore, *George Whitefield*, Wakeman, 1990

R E Davies, *I Will Pour Out My Spirit*, Monarch, 1992

J Deere, *Surprised by the Power of the Spirit*, Kingsway, 1994

B Edwards, *Revival*, Evangelical Press, 1990

J Edwards, *On Revival*, Banner, 1965. This volume includes the following works by the same author:
A Narrative of Surprising Conversions (1736)
Distinguishing Marks of a Work of the Spirit of God (1741)
An Account of the Revival in Northampton (1740–2, 1743)

J Edwards, *The Religious Affections*, Banner, 1986 (first published 1746)

J Edwards, *The Life and Diary of David Brainerd*, Moody, 1949 (first published 1749)

J Edwards, *The Works* (2 vols), Banner, 1974

D Erasmus (ed J Dolan), *The Essential Erasmus*, Meridian, 1964. This volume includes the following works by the same author:
Enchiridion (1503)
Praise of Folly (1509)

E Evans, *The Welsh Revival of 1904*, Evangelical Press of Wales, 1969

C Finney (ed K Johnson), *Lectures on Revival*, Bethany, 1988 (first published 1835)

C Finney (ed D Dayton), *Reflections on Revival*, Bethany, 1979 (first published 1845)

C Finney (ed H Wessel), *The Autobiography of Charles G Finney*, Bethany, 1977 (first published 1876)

E Gibbs, *I Believe in Church Growth*, Hodder, 1981

J Gordan, *Evangelical Spirituality*, SPCK, 1991

M Green, *Evangelism in the Early Church*, Hodder, 1970

M Green, *Evangelism – Now and Then*, IVP, 1979

M Green, *Evangelism Through the Local Church*, Hodder, 1990

M Green, *Acts for Today*, Hodder, 1993

H Harris, *His Own Story*, Bridge, 1984 (first published 1791)

R Knox, *Enthusiasm*, OUP, 1950

K Latourette, *A History of Christianity* (2 vols, revised), Harper & Row, 1975

D M Lloyd-Jones, *Revival*, Marshalls, 1986

D M Lloyd-Jones, *The Puritans*, Banner, 1987

D M Lloyd-Jones, *The Life of Joy*, Hodder, 1993

D M Lloyd-Jones, *The Life of Peace*, Hodder, 1993

R Lovelance, *Dynamics of Spiritual Life*, Paternoster, 1979

R M M'Cheyne (ed A Bonar) *The Memoir and Remains*, Banner, 1966 (first published 1844)

A McGrath, *Evangelicalism and the Future of Christianity*, Hodder, 1994

I Murray, *The Puritan Hope,* Banner, 1971

I Murray, *D Martyn Lloyd-Jones* (2 vol biography): vol 1: *The First Forty Years*, Banner, 1982; vol 2: *The Fight of Faith*, Banner, 1990

I Murray, *Jonathan Edwards*, Banner, 1987

I Murray, *Revival and Revivalism*, Banner, 1994

S Neill, *A History of Christian Missions*, Penguin, 1964

M Noll, D Bebbington, G Rawlyk (eds), *Evangelicalism*, OUP, 1994

J I Packer, *Keep in Step with the Spirit*, IVP, 1984

J I Packer, *Among God's Giants*, Kingsway, 1991

R Pointer, *How Do Churches Grow?*, Marc, 1984

J Pollock, *Moody without Sankey*, Hodder, 1963

J Pollock, *Wilberforce*, Constable, 1977

J Pollock, *John Wesley*, Hodder, 1989

D Pytches, *Come, Holy Spirit*, Hodder, 1985

L Ravenhill, *Why Revival Tarries*, Bethany, 1959

T Sargent, *The Sacred Anointing*, Hodder, 1994

R Steer, *George Muller: Delighted in God*, Hodder, 1975

R Steer, *J Hudson Taylor*, Hodder, 1990

H Snyder, *New Wineskins*, Marshalls, 1975

H Snyder, *The Radical Wesley*, IVP, 1980

H Snyder, *Liberating the Church*, Marshalls, 1983

H Taylor, *Biography of J H Taylor*, Hodder, 1965

D Tidball, *Who are the Evangelicals?*, Marshalls, 1994

J Tracy, *The Great Awakening*, Banner, 1989 (first published 1842)

A Wallis, *In the Day of Thy Power*, CLC, 1956

P Wagner, *Strategies for Church Growth*, Marc, 1987

R Warner, *Rediscovering the Spirit*, Hodder, 1986

R Warner, *21st Century Church*, Hodder, 1994

D Watson, *I Believe in Evangelism*, Hodder, 1976

C G Weakley, *The Nature of Revival*, Bethany, 1987

C Wesley (ed T Dudley-Smith), *A Living Flame of Love*, SPCK, 1987

J Wesley (ed N Curnock), *Journal (abridged)*, Epworth, 1958

J & C Wesley (ed F Whaling), *Selected Writings and Hymns*, SPCK, 1981

J White, *When the Spirit Comes in Power*, Hodder, 1988

G Whitefield, *Journals*, Banner, 1960

J Wimber, *Power Evangelism*, Hodder, 1985